TEEN
ANXIETY
TOOLKIT

A PRACTICAL GUIDE TO MANAGING SCHOOL STRESS, SOCIAL PRESSURE, AND EVERYDAY ANXIETY

AISHA BROADWATER, PhD

Teen Anxiety Toolkit:
A Practical Guide to Managing School Stress,
Social Pressure, and Everyday Anxiety

Copyright © 2025 Aisha Broadwater, PhD

This book is a work of nonfiction intended for educational and informational purposes only. It is not a substitute for professional medical, psychological, or therapeutic advice. If you or someone you know is struggling with mental health challenges, please consult a licensed professional.

Published by Enchanted Owl Publishing

First Edition: 2025

ISBN: 979-8-9943330-0-6

Printed in the United States of America

DOWNLOAD THE APP

This book gives you tools to understand and manage anxiety. The **2 Minute Calm** app helps you use those tools in real time.

Inside the app, you will find:

- Quick calm check-ins
- Guided breathing and grounding tools
- Simple journaling prompts
- Support for school stress, social pressure, and everyday anxiety

Scan to access the 2 Minute Calm companion app

2minutecalm.com

The 2 Minute Calm app is intended for educational and self-support purposes only and is not a substitute for professional mental health care.

DEDICATION

To every teen who's facing anxiety with quiet courage, this book is
for you. You are brave, you are growing and you are never alone on
this journey. Let this book be a tool you can turn to not just
on your good days, but especially on the tough ones.

Aisha Broadwater, PhD

TABLE OF CONTENT

Introduction   6

Chapter 1: How to Use This Book   7

Chapter 2: What Anxiety Looks Like for Teens   10

Chapter 3: The Anxiety Check-In Quiz   29

Chapter 4: Forms of Anxiety   34

Chapter 5: Anxiety and the Body   40

Chapter 6: School Pressure & Academic Anxiety   44

Chapter 7: Social Stress & Fitting In   61

Chapter 8: Calming Techniques That Actually Work   68

Chapter 9: What Is CBT (Cognitive Behavioral Therapy)?   76

Chapter 10: What Is Mindfulness?   83

Chapter 11: Changing Your Thoughts   89

Chapter 12: Managing the Inner Critic   93

Chapter 13: When Things Feel Too Heavy   99

Chapter 14: Building a Support System   108

Chapter 15: Social Media & Self-Image   116

Chapter 16: Your Personalized Anxiety Toolkit   119

Conclusion + Resources   123

INTRODUCTION

Anxiety in your teenage years can feel overwhelming. Whether it's the pressure to keep up with school, the fear of being judged on social media, or the daily stress of navigating friendships, it's easy to feel like no one gets it. This book was written to change that.

This guide is not about pretending anxiety doesn't exist. It's about giving you real tools that work in real moments, the kinds of strategies you can use between classes, before a presentation, or after a tough day.

You might think everyone else has it together, but here's the truth: most people are dealing with something, even if they don't talk about it. Anxiety affects millions of teens. It's common, it's manageable, and it does not define you.

You don't have to read everything in order. Jump to what you need. Return to what works. This is your space.

Let's get started.

CHAPTER 1

HOW TO USE THIS BOOK

This book isn't just something you read once and forget. It's a guide, a toolkit, and a companion. Whether you're dealing with daily stress, overwhelming anxiety, or simply trying to understand your feelings better, this book is here to walk with you, not talk at you. Let's break down how to use it in a way that makes sense for you.

1. This is Not a Textbook- It's a Toolkit

You won't find long lectures or boring explanations here. What you will find are strategies, reflections, exercises, and real-life tools that work. This isn't about memorizing facts; it's about learning how to take care of your mental health in ways that are practical and doable.

- **Read at Your Own Pace:** You don't have to read this book cover to cover. Start where you need help the most.

- **Use It Like a Toolkit:** Some chapters are like a first-aid kit for your brain. Others are more like a gym, where you build strength over time.

- **Repeat When Needed:** If something helps you once, return to it again. Repetition isn't failure, it's practice.

2. Reflect, Don't Just Read

At the end of each chapter, you'll find reflection questions and an action step. These are designed to help you process what you've learned and apply it to your own life.

- **Jot Down Your Thoughts:** Writing things down can help you make sense of your feelings.

- **Be Honest:** No one else is reading this but you. Say what you really feel, not what you think you should feel.

- **Track Your Progress:** You might be surprised how much you grow when you look back.

3. Build Your Personalized Anxiety Toolkit

Each chapter gives you tools, breathing techniques, ways to challenge thoughts, methods for handling social pressure, and more. The goal isn't to use every single one, but to find what works best for you.

- **Try One Tool at a Time:** Don't overwhelm yourself by trying to fix everything overnight.

- **Make a "Go-To" List:** As you find things that work, write them down in one place.

- **Use Your Toolkit Daily:** These tools aren't just for emergencies. Use them to build resilience over time.

Final Thought

This book doesn't promise to cure anxiety overnight. What it does offer is something far more powerful: the tools to face anxiety with clarity, confidence, and compassion. It's not a one-time fix, but a steady guide you can return to whenever you need it. Whether your anxiety feels like a constant or only shows up in certain moments, you now have ways to understand it and respond to it in a healthier way.

You don't have to wait for a crisis to open these pages. In fact, the most powerful changes often begin when you use your tools consistently, even on the average days. The small moments, the deep breaths, the grounding exercises, the quiet affirmations, are where real growth happens. They build your resilience one choice at a time. They remind your brain and body that you're safe, capable, and not alone.

Your journey with anxiety will have ups and downs. There will be good days where you feel strong and in control. And there will be harder days, when old patterns sneak back in or emotions feel heavy. That's okay. You're human. Progress isn't linear but it is real. Every step you take toward understanding yourself, setting boundaries, or choosing calm is a victory worth celebrating.

Let this book be more than just something you read once and shelve. Let it be your flashlight in the fog, your steady voice when your inner critic gets loud, and your reminder that healing isn't only possible, but it's already happening. You're doing the work, even if it doesn't always feel like it. Simply showing up you're moving forward.

This journey isn't about becoming perfect. It's about becoming more fully yourself. Through this process, you're learning one of life's most valuable truths: anxiety doesn't have to control your story. You are the one who shapes it.

This book is a small companion for a big journey, and choosing to open it even once is a monumental step in the right direction. Keep going. You are worth every ounce of effort it takes to heal.

Aisha Broadwater, PhD

CHAPTER 2

WHAT ANXIETY LOOKS LIKE FOR TEENS

What is Anxiety, really?

Anxiety isn't just something that happens before a big test or a social event. For many teens, it shows up daily in subtle, overwhelming, and often misunderstood ways. This chapter helps you understand what anxiety looks like during the teenage years, how it feels in your body, how it changes your thinking, and how to recognize when it's something more than just everyday stress.

Anxiety is your brain's way of trying to protect you. It's a survival response, a mental alarm system that tells you something might be wrong. Thousands of years ago, this alarm kept humans alive. If there was a rustle in the bushes, it could have been a predator, so the brain sent out a full-body alert: heart rate increased, muscles tensed, adrenaline surged. This reaction prepared your ancestors to fight, flee, or freeze, whatever it took to survive. That system still exists in your brain today, and it's powerful.

But the threats we face now are very different. Most of us aren't running from wild animals anymore. Instead, our "danger" comes in the form of modern stressors: a looming deadline, an awkward social interaction, a difficult family situation, or not getting a reply to a message. The problem is that your brain can't always tell the difference between real, physical danger and emotional or social discomfort. It reacts to both as if your safety is at risk.

That's why your body responds the way it does, with a racing heart, shallow breathing, an upset stomach, or sweaty palms, even when nothing life-threatening is happening.

This is called a "false alarm," and it's extremely common in people with anxiety. It doesn't mean something's wrong with you. It means your brain is trying to protect you, but it's firing too often or too intensely. It's like having an overly sensitive smoke detector that goes off when you burn toast. The alarm isn't trying to hurt you, it's just doing its job too well.

When your brain perceives a threat, it sends signals through a part of your nervous system called the **amygdala**, which is responsible for detecting danger. The amygdala doesn't take time to analyze the situation logically. It acts fast. Once it does, your body floods with stress hormones like cortisol and adrenaline. That's why you might feel jittery, hyperaware, or unable to think straight. Your body is preparing for action, not reflection.

Unfortunately, in everyday situations like giving a presentation, meeting someone new, or facing a tough conversation, this reaction can make things feel worse. Your brain thinks it's helping you, but it's actually increasing your discomfort. The truth is, the things that trigger anxiety today often need calm thinking, not emergency responses.

Understanding this can be empowering. If you can recognize that your anxiety is your brain's overprotective response, you can start to create space between the feeling and the reaction. You can say, "Okay, my brain is sounding an alarm. But is this really dangerous, or is it just uncomfortable?" That small pause gives you the chance to respond rather than react.

You're wired to survive. With awareness and the right tools, you can retrain your alarm system.

You can teach your brain that a hard conversation isn't the same as a tiger in the woods and that you are safe, even when you feel uncomfortable. That's what this book is about: learning to work with your brain, not against it.

Your brain is still under construction, especially the parts that control emotions and decision-making. That means your reactions might feel bigger, faster, or harder to manage.

It's More Than Just Worry

Worry is a part of life. It is something everyone experiences. A little bit of worry before a test, a game, or big event is totally normal and sometimes even helpful. It can push you to study harder, focus more, or take something seriously.

Anxiety is different. It's not just a passing thought or a brief moment of concern. It lingers. It loops. It starts to interfere with your ability to enjoy life or handle everyday situations. Think of worry like a passing cloud, it floats in, hangs around a bit, and then moves on. Anxiety, on the other hand, is more like a fog that rolls in and doesn't lift. It's persistent. It shows up even when there's no clear reason for it to. Instead of helping you prepare or perform, it starts to weigh you down.

One of the biggest signs that anxiety is more than just worry is how it affects your body. You might notice tension in your shoulders, stomachaches that won't go away, or a racing heart that kicks in for no clear reason. These physical symptoms are real, even if you can't always explain them. Anxiety lives in the body as much as it does in the mind. You may feel restless, easily startled, or constantly on edge, like you're waiting for something bad to happen. This kind of ongoing physical stress can be exhausting, especially when it feels like you can't turn it off.

Emotionally, anxiety also shows up in ways that can be hard to describe. You may avoid things you used to enjoy, stop reaching out to friends, or feel overwhelmed by small decisions. Your thoughts may race or spiral, imagining worst-case scenarios, replaying awkward moments, or worrying about how you come across to others. These thoughts don't just pop in and out; they stick. They repeat, and hey grow louder the more you try to ignore them. That's when anxiety starts to impact your day-to-day functioning.

For some people, anxiety might mean avoiding entire situations, like skipping school because of a presentation, not going to a party for fear of being judged, or putting off assignments because the pressure feels unbearable. Over time, this avoidance can shrink your world. It makes things feel harder and reinforces the belief that you can't handle them. That's how anxiety builds, it feeds on fear, avoidance, and silence.

And let's not forget sleep. One of the most common signs that anxiety has crossed the line from worry to something more serious is when it starts interrupting your ability to rest. You lie in bed, exhausted, but your mind won't slow down. You replay conversations, imagine what could go wrong tomorrow, or think about things that happened months ago. Sleep becomes something you dread instead of look forward to.

The truth is, anxiety isn't just about feeling nervous, it's about feeling stuck. It's about carrying a weight that others might not see but you feel every day. Recognizing that difference is the first step toward finding relief. You're not overreacting. You're not being dramatic. Most importantly, you're not alone.

Physical Symptoms and Why They Matter

One of the most confusing parts of anxiety is how it shows up in your body. A lot of teens think anxiety is only about racing thoughts or feeling nervous, but anxiety can affect you physically just as much as mentally and sometimes even more. If you've ever had a headache that wouldn't go away, a stomachache before school, or felt totally exhausted for no clear reason, there's a chance your anxiety was part of the cause.

For example, if your stomach always hurts in the morning, it might not be something you ate, it could be anxiety about school or social stress. If you get frequent headaches, especially tension headaches, they might be caused by tight muscles and constant worrying. If you're tired all the time, even after sleeping eight hours, your brain might be working overtime with anxious thoughts, preventing your body from truly resting.

The tricky part is that many teens (and even adults) don't connect these physical symptoms to anxiety. They might go to the doctor for a stomachache or dizziness, only to be told "everything looks normal." That can feel frustrating, like no one understands what's really going on. But here's the truth: just because something doesn't show up on a medical test doesn't mean it isn't real. Anxiety symptoms are real. Your body is reacting to something, and it deserves to be taken seriously.

Understanding this connection between your mind and body can be empowering. It means that when your body is sending you signals such as tight chest, a racing heart, or a clenched jaw, it's not betraying you. It's trying to alert you that something's off. Instead of ignoring those signals or feeling ashamed of them, you can learn to listen. You can ask: What am I feeling right now? What's stressing me out?

It also means that working on your mental health through breathing exercises, journaling, therapy, or calming routines can help your physical health too. You might find that once you manage your anxiety, your stomachaches decrease, your energy returns, or your headaches become less intense.

Key Insight:

When your body speaks, listen. Your anxiety might be using your body to get your attention. Don't push those signals aside. Honor them, and use them as a guide toward what needs care and attention.

Social Withdrawal or Irritability

You might cancel plans, stop texting back, or lash out when you're overwhelmed. These aren't just bad moods, they're often signs your anxiety is taking over. What may look like rudeness, disinterest, or "moodiness" from the outside is often your body's way of trying to manage emotional overload.

When anxiety builds up, your nervous system goes into protection mode. One way it does that is by pulling back from things that feel overwhelming, like socializing. Hanging out with friends might usually be something you enjoy, but when your mind is racing or your chest feels tight, even small interactions can feel exhausting. Canceling plans becomes a way to avoid the emotional toll of trying to act "normal" when you don't feel okay. Not responding to texts isn't about being careless, it's about feeling too drained to keep up.

Sometimes, instead of going quiet, anxiety shows up as anger or irritability. That might look like snapping at your sibling for asking a simple question, or feeling overly annoyed by a group chat that's blowing up your phone. You might even surprise yourself with how quickly your mood can shift from calm to explosive. This happens because anxiety creates tension not just in your thoughts, but in

your whole body. When that tension doesn't have a release, it can spill out as frustration, even over things that wouldn't normally bother you.

The tough part is that these behaviors often get misunderstood. You might be labeled as "lazy," "antisocial," or "dramatic," when in reality, you're dealing with emotions that feel too big to manage. This can lead to guilt, shame, or self-doubt which only fuels your anxiety more. It's a cycle that's hard to break unless someone recognizes what's really going on.

It's important to understand that anxiety doesn't always look like nervousness or panic. Sometimes it looks like avoidance. Sometimes it looks like being short-tempered. And sometimes it looks like silence. But beneath all of those reactions is the same core issue: your mind is trying to cope with a perceived threat, whether it's fear of judgment, failure, or simply not being able to keep up.

One of the best things you can do is learn to spot these patterns in yourself. Ask: "Am I pulling away because I need space, or because I'm overwhelmed and afraid I won't be enough?" "Am I irritable because someone's actually being annoying, or because I'm mentally overloaded and my tolerance is low?" Self-awareness doesn't fix everything, but it gives you the power to respond differently next time.

It's also helpful to let the people close to you know what anxiety looks like for you. You don't have to share every detail, but saying something like, "If I go quiet, it usually means I'm anxious, not mad," can make a big difference. The more you understand your own reactions, the more control you'll have over them and the more space you'll make for healing. Making friends doesn't require being popular it just takes connection.

How to Start:

- Join clubs, sports, or activities where you'll meet people with shared interests.

- Say something kind or ask a small question, such as, "Have you had this teacher before?

- Be yourself, even if that means being quiet at first.

Key Insight:

You don't need one hundred friends. One or two solid, safe people can change everything.

Dealing with Peer Pressure

Peer pressure isn't always loud. It doesn't always sound like "Do this or else you won't be cool." Sometimes, it's much quieter; a look, a laugh, a text thread you feel you should respond to in a certain way. It can be as subtle as feeling the need to wear a certain brand, pretend to like a show you don't, or say yes when your gut is screaming no. Because it's so quiet, it can be hard to recognize when it's happening.

As a teen, your brain is wired to care about social acceptance. That's normal. In fact, it's a survival mechanism from our early ancestors. Being accepted by the group meant safety. In today's world, this wiring can make it feel like every interaction is high-stakes. You may worry: "If I say no, will they think I'm weird? If I don't join in, will I get left out?" That fear is real, but giving in to it over and over can take you further away from who you truly are.

Here's the tricky thing about peer pressure: it often disguises itself as a desire to connect. You want to belong, and sometimes that means going along with things that don't align with your values, boundaries, or comfort level. You might laugh at a joke that feels wrong. You might go to a party you don't want to be at. You might pretend something doesn't bother you. Afterward, you're left with this uncomfortable feeling that you betrayed yourself a little.

The good news is, recognizing that discomfort is the first sign that you're becoming more self-aware. It means your internal compass is working. The more you listen to it, the stronger it gets.

One way to start dealing with peer pressure is to name it when it happens, even if you only do this in your mind. "I'm feeling pressure to say yes right now because I don't want to seem boring." Once you've named it, you can make a conscious choice rather than a reactive one. Ask yourself: *If I were alone right now, what would I choose?* That question helps strip away the noise and center your own voice.

Another strategy is to plan ahead. If you know a situation might test your boundaries, think through your response in advance. For example, if friends might pressure you to skip class or try something that makes you uneasy, rehearse a few lines you can use:

- "I'm good, thanks."

- "That's not really my thing."

- "Nah, I've got other plans."

You don't owe a long explanation. A short, confident response is enough.

17

Also, remember that you're not the only one feeling this way. Chances are, others in your group are also navigating their own version of peer pressure. Sometimes, being the first to say "no" gives others permission to do the same. You become a quiet leader, not because you're trying to control anyone, but because you're choosing to respect yourself.

Finally, reflect afterward. Did you stay true to yourself? If not, what would you do differently next time? Every experience is a chance to grow stronger in your values and clearer in your choices.

Key Insight:

Peer pressure loses power when you know who you are. The more often you choose what's right for *you*, the more confident and free you will feel.

Forms of Peer Pressure:

- Direct: "Come on, just do it."

- Subtle: Everyone else is doing it and no one questions it.

- Digital: Dares, trends, or pressure in group chats.

How to Say No Without Drama:

- Use humor: "I'd rather not fail this week, thanks though."

- Blame someone else: "My mom would seriously kill me."

- Be direct: "That's not for me."

When you know what you stand for, it's easier to say no.

Ask yourself:

- What kind of person do I want to be?

- Will I regret this later?

- Is this worth the stress?

Reflection Questions:

1. What social situations make you feel most anxious?

2. Are there any current friendships that feel more harmful than helpful?

3. What values are important to you in a friendship?

Action Step:

Write down three social strengths you have (e.g., "I'm a good listener," "I care about people," "I try to include others"). Then, write one small goal for building a new or stronger connection this month.

Hormones and Emotions

If you've ever felt totally fine one moment and then irritated, sad, or anxious the next for no obvious reason, you're not imagining things. Hormones play a big role in how we experience and process emotions, especially during the teen years. Understanding what's going on in your body can help you feel less confused and more in control.

Hormones are chemical messengers in your body. They help regulate everything from your appetite and sleep to your energy and emotions. During adolescence, your body begins producing more of certain hormones, like estrogen, testosterone, and cortisol. These changes are part of growing up, but they also create emotional turbulence. It's like your brain and body are in the middle of a major system upgrade, and there are a few glitches while things recalibrate.

One of the biggest hormonal changes that affects anxiety is the increase in cortisol, often called the "stress hormone." Cortisol is helpful in small doses because it helps your body react to danger and gives you energy. When you're constantly under stress, or your body is misreading safe situations as dangerous (as it often does in anxiety), cortisol can flood your system. Too much cortisol over time makes you feel tired, irritable, and emotionally drained. It can also make it harder to sleep, concentrate, or feel calm even when nothing stressful is happening.

Sleep is another area where hormones make a huge impact. As a teen, your sleep-wake cycle naturally shifts. Your body may not feel tired until later at night, but you still have to get up early for school, creating a mismatch. That ongoing lack of sleep lowers your brain's ability to manage emotions and increases your sensitivity to stress. In other words, when you're running on empty, your anxiety and emotional reactions become much harder to manage.

Mood swings are also common during this time. Hormonal fluctuations can cause feelings of sadness, frustration, or even panic to appear out of nowhere. This doesn't mean something is wrong with you, it means your body is adjusting. These emotional shifts can feel like waves. They rise, crash, and pass. The key is learning how to ride those waves instead of getting swept away.

If you've ever wondered, *"Why am I crying right now?"* or *"Why did I just snap at someone when I wasn't even mad two minutes ago?"* hormones could be part of the answer. These mood shifts aren't excuses, but they are explanations. When you understand what's happening inside you, you can meet your emotions with more patience instead of judgment.

Key Insight: Your changing hormones are not your enemy. They're doing their job. During this phase of life, they can amplify feelings, making small things feel huge. The more you learn to recognize these patterns, the more power you have to respond with awareness rather than frustration.

So the next time you feel overwhelmed for "no reason," pause and ask yourself: *Could this be my body processing something?* The answer might surprise you and bring a little more compassion into how you treat yourself.

Breaking the Myths

One of the hardest parts about struggling with anxiety is not just the symptoms themselves, it's the misunderstanding that surrounds them. Myths and misconceptions about anxiety can make teens feel like what they're experiencing isn't valid, important, or worthy of help. That kind of invisibility makes everything harder. Let's break down some of the most common myths and replace them with truth.

Myth 1: "It's All in Your Head"

If you've ever opened up about your anxiety and heard someone say, *"It's all in your head,"* you're not alone. People often say this as a way to comfort or dismiss, but it can be deeply invalidating. What they may not realize is that anxiety isn't *just* in your head, it's in your body, your thoughts, your emotions, and your daily life. It's a full-body experience, and reducing it to a simple thought pattern overlooks the complexity of what you're going through.

Hearing "It's all in your head" can also make you feel like you just need to "think more positively" to feel better. While shifting your mindset is a powerful tool, it's not a magic switch. Anxiety isn't something you snap out of, it's something you work through. That work involves understanding your triggers, using calming strategies, and practicing tools that help you regulate both mind and body. Minimizing it makes that process harder and more isolating.

When someone listens and says, *"That sounds really hard. I'm here for you,"* it doesn't erase the anxiety, but it makes the burden lighter. You don't need someone to fix you. You need someone to understand.

So, the next time someone tells you it's all in your head, you can remind yourself of the truth: Anxiety lives in your whole system. It's real, it matters, and healing starts when it's acknowledged, not denied.

Myth 2: "I'm Just Being Dramatic"

Many teens grow up hearing that they're overreacting or being too emotional when they express fear, overwhelm, or sadness. Anxiety isn't drama, it's a genuine emotional and physiological response to stress. Calling someone "dramatic" invalidates their experience and teaches them to hide their feelings rather than process them. Over time, this builds shame, silence, and self-doubt.

The truth is, when your emotions feel huge, it's because your nervous system is on high alert. Teens especially are in a unique developmental window where the brain is still growing, emotions run high, and identity is being shaped. Feeling big emotions is part of growing. Having anxiety doesn't make you dramatic; it makes you human.

Myth 3: "Everyone Else Is Fine"

One of the most isolating lies anxiety tells is that you're the only one struggling. You scroll through social media and see people smiling, succeeding, hanging out with friends and it feels like they have it all together while you're falling apart. But here's what you don't see: their fears, doubts, and worries that they don't post.

Social media is a highlight reel, not a reality show. Everyone filters what they show. The truth is, many people your age are dealing with similar struggles panic attacks before exams, trouble sleeping, overthinking messages, and more. You're not weird. You're just seeing behind the curtain of your own life while only viewing the polished front stage of others.

The more we talk about mental health, the more we realize how many of us are dealing with the same things in silence. Breaking this myth starts with honesty with yourself and with others. You never know who might breathe a sigh of relief when you speak up and say, "Me too."

Why Validation Matters

When you're anxious, what you need most isn't always advice or solutions. Often it's *validation*. That simple act of someone saying, "I hear you. What you're feeling makes sense," can create more relief than a hundred suggestions. Why? Because validation tells your brain and body: *You're safe now.*

Let's unpack why this is so powerful.

Anxiety often feels like your internal alarm system is stuck in the "on" position. Your heart races, your thoughts spiral, and you might feel completely alone in your worry. When someone shows you empathy, your nervous system responds. Research has shown that emotional validation especially from a trusted person can actually reduce stress levels, slow your breathing, and help your mind settle. It's not magic. It's biology. Feeling seen and heard helps your body return to a place of calm.

For teens especially, validation is critical. You're in a stage of life where you're figuring out who you are, where you belong, and how you want to be treated. When someone brushes off your experience with, "You're overreacting," "It's not a big deal," or "You'll be fine," it can cause you to doubt your own reality. You may start to think your feelings don't matter or worse, that you're broken for having them. Over time, this can lead to silence, shame, or even more intense anxiety.

Validation doesn't mean someone agrees with everything you say or feel. It simply means they accept that your feelings are real and important. For example, if you say, "I'm freaking out about this math test," a validating response might be, "It sounds like this is really stressing you out. I can understand why that feels overwhelming." They're not trying to solve the test. They're giving you space to be human.

Unfortunately, many people skip validation and jump straight to problem-solving. They might say, "Just study harder," or "You'll do fine," thinking they're helping. Without validation first, advice can feel like pressure. Before your brain can take in logic, it needs to feel safe. Validation is how you open that door.

And here's something empowering you can also validate *yourself*. You don't have to wait for someone else to say the right thing. Practice saying to yourself, "It makes sense that I feel anxious right now," or "This is a lot, and it's okay that I'm struggling." These small, compassionate thoughts create an internal sense of safety. Self-validation helps you build resilience from the inside out.

So, the next time anxiety shows up, and you find yourself spiraling, remember: the first step isn't always to fix it. The first step is to acknowledge it. To say, "I see you, I hear you, and you're not crazy for feeling this way." That moment of recognition might be the calm your mind needs to move forward.

Validation matters because you matter. And feeling understood is one of the first steps toward healing.

Self-Doubt and Minimizing Your Struggles

It starts small: you feel overwhelmed, anxious, or upset, and then you immediately question yourself. *"Maybe I'm just being too sensitive." "Other people have it worse." "I should be able to handle this."* That's the voice of self-doubt. When it shows up often enough, you start to believe that your feelings don't deserve space.

If you've ever been told to "toughen up," "stop being dramatic," or "quit crying over nothing," you've likely internalized the message that your emotions are a problem. That message might not have been said to hurt you, but it teaches you to second-guess your emotional responses. Over time, this can lead to minimizing your own struggles even when what you're facing is genuinely hard.

Here's the truth: feeling something deeply doesn't make you weak. It means you're connected to your inner world. Sensitivity isn't a flaw, it's a signal. It shows you care. It shows you notice. It shows that your nervous system responds strongly to emotional input and that's not something to be ashamed of.

Minimizing your struggles often comes from comparing your pain to others'. You might think, *"Other people have real problems, so I shouldn't complain."* But pain isn't a competition. Just because someone else is struggling doesn't mean your experience matters less. You wouldn't tell someone with a broken arm to "be grateful they didn't lose the whole arm." Struggles are valid even if someone else is also struggling. Your emotions deserve acknowledgment without being measured against others'.

When you doubt your right to feel what you're feeling, you suppress your natural need for support. You might not speak up when something is wrong, or you might pretend to be okay even when you're not. This creates a cycle, because the less you express what's going on, the more isolated you feel. And the more isolated you feel, the more likely you are to believe that your emotions don't matter.

You can break this cycle. It starts with self-compassion. Instead of saying, *"This isn't a big deal,"* try asking, *"Why does this feel big to me?"* Instead of pushing your feelings down, practice writing them out or sharing them with someone you trust. Naming your experience is a huge step toward healing.

It also helps to build a new kind of inner voice, one that gently challenges the self-doubt. When that critical thought appears (*"I'm just being sensitive"*), you can respond with, *"Maybe I am sensitive. And that's okay. It means I'm aware of what matters to me."* When you start treating your emotions like messengers instead of nuisances, you'll realize that sensitivity is a strength. It's what allows you to connect, care, and grow.

You don't have to justify your struggles to anyone, not even to yourself. They're real. They're worth understanding. They're signs that something inside you is asking to be heard.

"I'm Just Being Dramatic"

How many times have you felt overwhelmed, only to follow it up with the thought, *"Maybe I'm just being dramatic"*? Maybe you were crying over something others called "small," or your heart was pounding over a situation your friends thought was "no big deal." That voice of self-doubt can creep in fast, especially if others have ever made you feel like your emotions are "too much."

Dismissing your own experience with phrases like *"I'm overreacting"* or *"It's not that serious"* is actually one of anxiety's sneakiest tricks. Anxiety often distorts your thinking. It tells you you're exaggerating, even when your response is completely valid for what you're going through. And when you tell yourself your feelings don't count, you silence the part of you that needs care and understanding the most.

Let's reframe this: big emotions are signals, not flaws. If your stomach is in knots before school, or you cry after a tough conversation, or you feel physically exhausted by social situations that's not drama. That's your nervous system speaking up. Your body and mind are trying to tell you that something feels unsafe, uncertain, or too heavy to hold alone. You wouldn't call someone dramatic for limping when they've hurt their leg. Emotional pain deserves the same compassion.

Still, it's common to feel pressure to "toughen up" or "get over it," especially if people around you don't understand anxiety. When your feelings are dismissed by others, like parents, teachers, or even friends, it's easy to internalize that message. You may start to believe that asking for support is attention-seeking. But pushing your feelings down doesn't make them go away. It often makes them grow louder.

Emotional overwhelm is not a character flaw. It's a cue. It's your body saying, *"Hey, something's not okay here."* Ignoring that doesn't make you stronger. Listening to it, then choosing to respond with kindness and action is where true strength lives.

So next time the voice in your head says, *"I'm just being dramatic,"* pause and check in. What are you really feeling? What triggered it? What do you need right now? That kind of self-honesty is emotional intelligence.

Trusting Your Feelings

One of the hardest parts of dealing with anxiety is learning to trust your own feelings, especially when they don't always make sense to the people around you. You may wonder: *Is this a real problem? Am I overreacting? Should I just ignore this and move on?* But your feelings aren't random. They exist for a reason. Even when they're confusing or intense, they're giving you valuable information about what's going on inside you.

Feelings are like your body's emotional dashboard, they light up when something needs attention. Just as physical pain alerts you to an injury, emotional pain tells you that something in your environment or inner world is out of balance. Maybe you're overwhelmed, stretched too thin, not being heard, or facing pressure that doesn't feel fair. Anxiety might be your brain's way of saying, *something about this situation isn't sitting right.*

The challenge is that we live in a culture that often encourages people especially teens, to push past emotions. You might hear things like *"Just ignore it,"* or *"It's not a big deal."* Over time, those messages can cause you to doubt yourself. You might start depending on others to tell you how to feel or what to do. But here's the truth: you don't need someone else to approve your experience for it to be real.

If your heart is racing in class, if your stomach twists before a social event, or if you feel uneasy around a certain person or place, those feelings matter. They're signals. Trusting your feelings doesn't mean you let anxiety run the show. It means you take your emotions seriously enough to listen to them and explore what they're telling you. You ask, *What might I need right now?*

Learning to trust your feelings takes practice. Start small. If you feel like you need a break, take one. If a conversation makes you feel uncomfortable, it's okay to step away. If your gut tells you something's off, pause and pay attention. You may not always have immediate answers, but giving yourself permission to feel and reflect is the first step toward clarity.

It also helps to keep track of your emotions over time. Journaling or mood tracking can help you notice patterns and build confidence in your emotional awareness. The more you acknowledge your feelings, the more fluent you become in understanding them. This emotional fluency is a superpower, it allows you to navigate life with greater insight and intention.

You are the expert on your own experience. Others can offer guidance and support, but you are the one living it. Your feelings are not wrong, too much, or inconvenient. They are part of being human and they are worthy of your attention.

So, the next time someone tells you to brush it off, remember this: you're allowed to take your emotions seriously. Trusting your feelings is a form of wisdom. You have every right to listen to that wisdom.

Reflection Questions

- When does anxiety show up most for you: school, social events, nighttime?

- What myths or thoughts do you carry about anxiety that might not be true?

- Who could you talk to if you needed help with anxious feelings?

Action Step

Track your anxiety patterns for one week. Each night, write down:

1. One moment you felt anxious

2. What triggered it

3. How your body responded

4. What helped, even a little

CHAPTER 3

THE ANXIETY CHECK-IN QUIZ

Before we go deeper into managing anxiety, it helps to take a clear snapshot of how anxiety shows up in your life right now. This chapter provides a practical self-assessment quiz designed to help you reflect on your symptoms, stress triggers, and emotional responses.

This isn't about labeling yourself or putting yourself into a box. It's about creating awareness. The more clearly you understand your anxiety, the more effectively you can manage it.

Why Take an Anxiety Check-In Quiz?

Understanding your anxiety means you can respond, not just react. A quiz like this helps you:

- Spot patterns in your thoughts and behavior

- Notice physical symptoms tied to stress

- Identify which tools might be most useful for you later in the book

Key Insight:

Awareness isn't weakness. It's your first layer of strength. It allows you to name what's happening and choose a healthy response.

Instructions:

Read each question and answer honestly. Use the scale provided to rate how often the statement applies to you.

Scale:

0 – Never

1 – Rarely

2 – Sometimes

3 – Often

4 – Almost Always

Anxiety Check-In Quiz

1. I often feel nervous, worried, or on edge for no clear reason. [0–4]

2. I avoid situations (like school, social events, or new experiences) because of fear or anxiety. [0–4]

3. I have trouble falling asleep or staying asleep because of racing thoughts. [0–4]

4. I get headaches, stomachaches, or other physical symptoms when I'm anxious. [0–4]

5. I feel overwhelmed by small tasks or decisions. [0–4]

6. I replay past mistakes or embarrassing moments in my head. [0–4]

7. I worry about what others think of me almost every day. [0–4]

8. I find it hard to relax, even when I have nothing going on. [0–4]

9. I feel like something bad is going to happen, even when there's no real danger. [0–4]

10. I get irritated or emotional easily, especially when I'm under pressure. [0–4]

11. I avoid talking about how I feel because I don't want to burden others. [0–4]

12. I feel like I have to be perfect to be accepted or liked. [0–4]

13. I notice my heart racing, shallow breathing, or feeling shaky when anxious. [0–4]

14. I fear being judged, rejected, or embarrassed in front of others. [0–4]

15. I often feel tired, unmotivated, or emotionally drained. [0–4]

16. I worry about my future or constantly feel like I'm running out of time. [0–4]

17. I find myself overthinking conversations, texts, or social media posts. [0–4]

18. I feel like no one understands how anxious I really am. [0–4]

19. I try to hide my anxiety and pretend everything's fine. [0–4]

20. I wish I could feel more in control of my mind and emotions. [0–4]

Scoring Your Quiz:

1. 0–20: Low Anxiety – You may not experience anxiety often or it may be situational.

2. 21–40: Mild Anxiety – Anxiety may show up occasionally but doesn't interfere with daily life too much.

3. 41–60: Moderate Anxiety – Anxiety is a regular part of your week and affects how you think or feel.

4. 61–80: High Anxiety – Anxiety is likely affecting school, relationships, or overall well-being.

5. 81+: Severe Anxiety – Anxiety may feel overwhelming or constant. It's time to seek extra support.

Important Note:

This quiz is not a diagnosis. It's a self-check. If your score is high, talk to a counselor, therapist, or trusted adult. Anxiety is treatable, and you don't have to go through it alone.

Understanding Your Score

Mild Anxiety:

Even if anxiety is light, it still deserves attention. You can start with calming techniques, journaling, or basic mindfulness.

Moderate Anxiety:

This is where most teens fall. You'll benefit from learning coping strategies, setting boundaries, and talking to someone about what you're going through.

High to Severe Anxiety:

These levels can feel exhausting. You might struggle to function well at school, home, or in relationships. That doesn't mean something is wrong with you, it just means you need more tools and support.

How to Use This Information

- Keep a copy of your score in a journal. Over time, you'll track what helps and what doesn't.

- Identify your highest-rated areas. Do you notice physical symptoms? Racing thoughts? Avoidance behaviors?

- Use those areas to guide which chapters in this book to focus on.

Key Insight:

What gets measured gets managed. The more clearly you understand how anxiety affects you, the more power you have to make real changes.

Reflection Questions:

1. Which quiz questions felt most true for you?

2. What are the first signs that anxiety is building up in your life?

3. Who could you talk to about what you're experiencing?

Action Step:

Write down your top 3 anxiety triggers. Then write one healthy response you want to try the next time each one comes up. Keep this list somewhere visible, like in your room, journal, or school binder.

CHAPTER 4

FORMS OF ANXIETY

Anxiety doesn't look the same for everyone. It can sneak up as overthinking before a test, freeze you at a party, or keep you awake with racing thoughts. This chapter breaks down the most common forms of anxiety teens experience. By understanding the differences, you'll be better equipped to identify what's happening in your own mind and what to do about it.

Why This Matters

Not all anxiety is created equal. What helps with one kind of anxiety might not work for another. Knowing the type of anxiety, you're facing can lead to more targeted strategies and less self-blame.

Key Insight:

Naming your anxiety is powerful. When you know what you're dealing with, you can take it less personally and respond with clarity instead of fear.

1. Generalized Anxiety Disorder (GAD)

What It Feels Like:

GAD is like a constant hum of worry. You may feel anxious about school, the future, your health, your family, everything and nothing at once. These worries aren't always based on real problems, but they still feel heavy and real.

Common Signs:

- Persistent worry about multiple areas of life

- Feeling restless, irritable, or on edge

- Muscle tension, headaches, stomachaches

- Trouble concentrating or sleeping

How It Affects Teens:

GAD can make it hard to focus in class or enjoy time with friends. You may feel like you're always waiting for something bad to happen, even if things are fine on the outside.

2. Social Anxiety

What It Feels Like:

Social anxiety goes beyond shyness. It's a fear of being judged, embarrassed, or rejected in social situations. Even everyday interactions, like raising your hand in class or eating in front of others can feel terrifying.

Common Signs:

- Avoiding social events or conversations

- Worrying for days about an upcoming presentation or group activity

- Overanalyzing things you said or did after social interactions

- Blushing, sweating, shaking, or feeling frozen in public

How It Affects Teens:

You might skip school events, isolate yourself, or pretend to be sick to avoid attention. Social media might feel safer than real life. But the more you avoid, the harder social situations become.

3. Panic Disorder

What It Feels Like:

Panic disorder involves sudden, intense waves of fear called panic attacks. These can come out of nowhere and feel like something serious is wrong with your body even though you're safe.

Common Signs:

- Rapid heart rate, chest pain, or difficulty breathing

- Dizziness, nausea, or numbness

- Feeling detached from reality or yourself

- Fear of "going crazy" or dying

How It Affects Teens:

After one panic attack, you may start avoiding places or situations where it happened, fearing it will occur again. This fear of fear can become its own trap.

4. Separation Anxiety

What It Feels Like:

This isn't just something kids feel. Teens can experience intense anxiety when separated from loved ones or familiar environments.

Common Signs:

- Extreme distress about being away from home or family

- Refusing to go to school or sleep alone

- Frequent worry about something bad happening to loved ones

- Trouble concentrating or functioning when apart

How It Affects Teens:

You may feel embarrassed by your attachment or struggle with sleepovers, field trips, or the idea of leaving for college. This form of anxiety is often misunderstood but it's very real.

5. Specific Phobias

What It Feels Like:

Phobias are intense, irrational fears about specific objects or situations, like spiders, needles, elevators, or thunderstorms.

Common Signs:

- Immediate fear response when exposed to the trigger

- Avoiding the object/situation at all costs

- Physical symptoms (sweating, shaking, nausea)

- Disruption to your daily life or activities

How It Affects Teens:

Phobias can feel embarrassing, but they're surprisingly common. A fear doesn't have to make sense to be real and it can still be managed with the right tools.

6. Obsessive-Compulsive Disorder (OCD)

What It Feels Like:

OCD involves intrusive thoughts (obsessions) and behaviors or rituals (compulsions) that you feel driven to repeat in order to ease the anxiety.

Common Signs:

- Repetitive behaviors like handwashing, counting, or checking

- Fear that something bad will happen unless you do something "just right"

- Difficulty focusing because of looping thoughts

- Feeling frustrated or exhausted by your own mind

How It Affects Teens:

OCD can interfere with your schoolwork, sleep, or relationships. It's not just about being neat or organized it's about trying to feel safe in an anxious world.

7. Health Anxiety

What It Feels Like:

Also known as hypochondria, health anxiety is constant worry about having or developing a serious illness even if there's no evidence.

Common Signs:

- Constantly googling symptoms

- Fixating on normal body sensations

- Frequent doctor visits or reassurance-seeking

- Fear of catching or spreading illness

How It Affects Teens:

This form of anxiety can increase during flu season or after a health scare. You may struggle to trust your body or feel stuck in a loop of worry and checking.

8. Performance Anxiety

What It Feels Like:

Performance anxiety shows up when you're under pressure to succeed on stage, in sports, during exams, or in front of others.

Common Signs:

- Freezing during presentations or performances

- Negative self-talk before or after events

- Physical tension, nausea, or panic

- Perfectionism that blocks action

How It Affects Teens:

It can make you dread things you used to enjoy like drama club, debate team, or a soccer game. The fear of failure becomes bigger than the event itself.

Recognizing Patterns

Is your mind always running? Do you dread things you used to enjoy? Are you constantly tired or irritable? These may be signs your body is stuck in an anxious loop.

Putting It All Together

It's normal to experience more than one form of anxiety at the same time. You might deal with social anxiety and performance anxiety, or general worry mixed with health anxiety. The key is to notice your patterns and explore which tools work best for you.

Key Insight:

You don't need a label to deserve support. These descriptions are meant to help you understand, not to limit or define you.

Reflection Questions:

1. Which of these forms of anxiety felt most familiar to you?

2. How does anxiety usually show up in your body, thoughts, and behavior?

3. Is there a type of anxiety you want to understand or manage better?

Action Step:

Pick one form of anxiety from this chapter and do a mini-research session. Write down what it looks like for you, what you've tried in the past, and one new tool you'd like to try after reading the upcoming chapters.

CHAPTER 5

ANXIETY AND THE BODY

In an earlier chapter we touched on *Physical Symptoms and Why They Matter*, let's take a deeper dive here in this chapter and discuss anxiety and the body. Understanding the physical side of anxiety helps you recognize what's happening, respond to it with compassion, and gain a sense of control. This chapter explores how anxiety manifests physically, why it does that, and what you can do to calm your body when it's overwhelmed.

Why Anxiety Feels Physical

Your brain and body are constantly communicating. When you have a stressful thought, your brain sends signals to your body to prepare for danger. This is known as the fight-flight-freeze response.

The Fight-Flight-Freeze Response

Fight: You might feel angry, agitated, or ready to lash out. This response shows up when your brain thinks you need to confront a threat.

Flight: You may feel the urge to escape, leave the classroom, avoid a conversation, or run away from your responsibilities.

Freeze: You feel stuck. Your mind goes blank, your body feels heavy, and you can't seem to act or speak.

Physical Symptoms of Anxiety

1. Rapid Heartbeat: Your heart pumps faster to get more blood to your muscles preparing you to "fight or flee."

2. Shallow Breathing: You might breathe quickly and from your chest instead of your belly, leading to dizziness or chest tightness.

3. Stomach Issues: Anxiety often affects digestion, causing nausea, cramps, or a churning feeling in your gut.

4. Muscle Tension: Your shoulders, jaw, or back might tighten up as your body prepares for action.

5. Sweating and Shaking: These are natural ways your body releases tension and cools down during stress.

6. Headaches and Fatigue: Constant anxiety can exhaust your nervous system, leading to tension headaches and feeling drained.

Understanding the Nervous System

The autonomic nervous system has two parts:

- Sympathetic Nervous System: Triggers the fight-flight-freeze response.

- Parasympathetic Nervous System: Calms you down and restores balance.

The key to managing physical anxiety is learning how to activate your calming system, the parasympathetic nervous system.

Body-Based Tools for Calming Anxiety

1. **Deep Belly Breathing**: Breathe in slowly through your nose, expanding your belly, then exhale gently through your mouth. Repeat for a few minutes.

2. **Grounding Exercises:** Notice 5 things you can see, 4 you can touch, 3

3. you can hear, 2 you can smell, and 1 you can taste. This keeps your focus in the present.

4. **Progressive Muscle Relaxation:** Tense each muscle group for five seconds, then release. Start from your feet and work up to your head.

5. **Gentle Movement:** Walking, stretching, yoga, or dancing can release stored stress and soothe your system.

6. **Cold Water Technique:** Splashing cold water on your face or holding a cool object can reset your stress response.

How to Listen to Your Body

Your body sends signals long before your mind catches up. When you notice physical symptoms, ask yourself:

- What might I be feeling emotionally?
- Is there something stressful happening?
- What does my body need right now?

Key Insight:

Physical symptoms are messages, not enemies. They're telling you to pause, check in, and respond with care.

Common Misunderstandings

1. "I'm Sick": Anxiety can mimic illness, but if symptoms come and go with stress, they're likely anxiety-related.

2. "Something Is Wrong with Me." These symptoms are common, manageable, and valid.

3. "I Should Be Able to Control This": Anxiety is a body-brain response. You're not weak for experiencing it.

When to See a Doctor

If you're unsure whether your symptoms are anxiety or a medical issue, talk to a healthcare provider. It's always okay to ask. Getting clarity can actually ease your worry.

Creating a Body Awareness Plan

Step 1: Track Your Symptoms

Keep a simple journal of when physical symptoms show up and what's going on around you.

Step 2: Identify Triggers

Notice if patterns emerge before tests, after arguments, during social events, etc.

Step 3: Build a Soothing Routine

Create a list of go-to physical strategies that help you feel safe and calm.

Reflection Questions:

1. How does anxiety show up in your body?

2. Which physical symptoms do you tend to notice first?

3. What physical coping tools help you feel more in control?

Action Step:

Create a "Body Scan" routine. Once a day, take 3–5 minutes to sit quietly, breathe, and mentally check in with each part of your body. Write down anything you notice. Use this as a guide to tune in before anxiety spirals out of control.

CHAPTER 6

SCHOOL PRESSURE & ACADEMIC ANXIETY

You're expected to perform well in school, fit in socially, plan for your future, and somehow stay calm through it all. That's a lot, and anxiety often grows in the space between expectations and reality. What people don't always see is the invisible weight that teens carry. You're not just dealing with homework or friend drama; you're managing the pressure to succeed, to be liked, to get it all "right" in a world that doesn't always make space for mistakes.

Social and Academic Expectations

In school, it can feel like every grade matters. A single test can determine whether you're eligible for honors classes or a scholarship. That pressure builds quietly. Maybe you study late into the night and still feel behind. Or maybe you procrastinate because the thought of even starting gives you anxiety. The fear of failure doesn't just stay in the classroom, it comes home with you, follows you to bed, and wakes up with you the next morning.

Now add social expectations to that mix. Fitting in isn't as simple as finding people who like you. It can feel like a full-time job. There are unspoken rules about what to wear, how to act, who to be seen with, and what to post on social media. One wrong move, one awkward moment, and it can feel like your whole image is on the line. This constant social performance can be exhausting. It's no wonder your nervous system stays on high alert, your brain is trying to protect you from rejection, criticism, or being "othered."

And then, as if school and social pressure weren't enough, there's the future. Adults ask questions like, "What do you want to be?" or "Where are you going to college?" when you might not even know what you want for lunch today. The pressure to map out your life before you've even lived much of it is overwhelming. It makes anxiety feel like a ticking clock, counting down the time you have to figure everything out.

When expectations are high and support feels low, anxiety thrives. You may start to believe you're not doing enough, not smart enough, not likable enough. But the truth is: you are doing the best you can under immense pressure. What's often missing is acknowledgment of how hard it really is. You're not lazy. You're not overly sensitive. You're someone living through a very demanding phase of life, often without the emotional tools adults assume you already have.

Anxiety is a signal that the demands on you might be too much for your system to carry alone. When you start noticing those feelings, tight chest, racing thoughts, avoidance, perfectionism, don't brush them off. They're clues that you need support, not punishment. That you need understanding, not more pressure.

It's okay to slow down. It's okay to say you're overwhelmed. And it's more than okay to rewrite the rules that are making you anxious. Your value isn't found in your performance, it's found in your presence, your effort, and the courage it takes to keep going, even when it's hard.

School can be one of the biggest sources of anxiety for teens. Between grades, deadlines, extracurriculars, and expectations for the future, it's easy to feel overwhelmed. This chapter breaks down what academic anxiety looks like, where it comes from, and how to deal with it in healthy, practical ways.

Why School Feels So Overwhelming

For many teens, school is a major source of anxiety. Grades, expectations, assignments, presentations, it can feel like you're constantly being tested, not just on paper, but in life. This chapter will help you break down the pressure, build realistic coping strategies, and take back a sense of control.

School isn't just about learning, it's where you spend most of your day, where you're evaluated, and where you're often compared to others. The fear of failure or not measuring up can make even the most capable students feel anxious or stuck.

Key Insight:

Academic anxiety doesn't mean you're incapable. It means your nervous system needs a better strategy for managing the stress.

The Pressure to Perform

You may feel:

- Like your future depends on every test

- Constant guilt for not doing "enough"

- A fear of disappointing others or yourself

These thoughts can create a feedback loop that increases procrastination and self-doubt.

Homework Overwhelm

Homework stress can feel endless. When you're already mentally drained, even simple tasks can feel overwhelming.

Strategies:

- Break tasks into small chunks

- Use a timer (like 25 minutes on, 5 minutes off)

- Prioritize by deadline and importance

Coping with Overwhelm

When anxiety peaks, your brain can't function clearly. Here's how to reset:

Recognize the Signs:

- You avoid everything
- You snap at people
- You feel exhausted just thinking about school

Reset Rituals:

- Take a short walk or stretch
- Use breathing or grounding tools
- Write down everything you need to do, then pick one task

Asking for Academic Help

Many teens avoid asking for help out of fear of looking "dumb." In reality, reaching out is a strength.

How to ask:

- Talk to teachers about confusing material early
- Use office hours or peer tutors
- If needed, ask a counselor about accommodations

Key Insight:

Struggling with a subject doesn't mean you're failing as a person. Learning isn't linear and help exists for a reason.

After-School Routines:

- Set a time to stop doing schoolwork
- Plan one small fun or relaxing activity each evening
- Avoid screens right before bed

Managing Extracurriculars

It's great to be involved, but not at the expense of your mental health.

Tips:

- Choose a few things you enjoy (not everything)

- Learn to say "no" without guilt

- Build in breaks between activities

Planning for the Week

Sunday scaries are real. Instead of dreading the week, prep for it with a calm mindset.

Ideas:

- Lay out clothes or pack your bag ahead of time

- Review your calendar so nothing surprises you

- Schedule something fun to look forward to mid-week

Reflection Questions:

1. What part of school causes you the most anxiety?

2. How do you usually cope with academic stress and how is that working?

3. Who could you ask for support when school starts to feel too big?

Action Step:

Create a "School Stress Toolkit." Include 3 things that calm you when overwhelmed, 2 people you can talk to, and 1 phrase to remind yourself (like: "This grade doesn't define me").

Test Anxiety: What It Feels Like and Why It Happens

Test anxiety isn't just "nerves." It can be a full-body experience. Your heart races, your stomach tightens, your thoughts scatter. You might study for hours, only to blank out the moment you see the first question. For some teens, the pressure to succeed is so intense that it triggers a fear-based response that makes it hard to think clearly, let alone perform at your best.

At its core, test anxiety is often fueled by fear: fear of failure, fear of letting down your parents or teachers, or fear of not living up to the expectations you've placed on yourself. Recognizing that fear is the first step toward taking back control.

So, what can you do about it?

1. Prepare, Don't Cram

One of the biggest sources of test anxiety is feeling unprepared. Cramming the night before increases stress and reduces retention.

What to Try:

Spread out your study time: Start studying several days in advance using short, focused sessions (20–30 minutes) instead of one long stretch.

- **Use practice questions:** Simulating the test environment helps your brain feel more comfortable when the real test comes.

- **Create a study schedule:** Break the material into smaller parts and assign them to specific days.

2. Use Calming Techniques Before and During the Test

Your nervous system needs a signal that you're safe. Physical techniques can send that signal quickly.

What to Try:

- **Box breathing:** Inhale for 4 counts, hold for 4, exhale for 4, hold for 4. Repeat until your body begins to calm.

- **Progressive muscle relaxation:** Tense and then release each muscle group starting at your toes and working up.

- **Positive self-talk:** Replace "I'm going to fail" with "I've prepared for this. I can do hard things."

3. Talk to Your Teacher

Believe it or not, teachers want you to succeed. If you're struggling with test anxiety, talk to them ahead of time.

What to Try:

- **Ask for clarification:** If certain types of questions make you panic, ask if there are alternative formats.

- **Get extra time or quiet space:** Some schools offer accommodations for students with anxiety, ask your counselor

- **Share how you feel:** You don't have to give every detail, just something like: "I've been having a tough time with anxiety during tests."

4. Build Pre-Test Rituals

What you do the morning of the test can shape how your brain and body respond.

What to Try:

- **Get good sleep the night before.** Lack of rest heightens stress hormones.

- **Eat something balanced.** Fuel your body with protein and complex carbs, not just sugar.

- **Avoid last-minute cramming.** This usually increases panic instead of building confidence.

5. Reframe the Meaning of the Test

When you attach your self-worth to your grades, every test feels like a personal judgment. That mindset can be crippling.

What to Try:

- **Remind yourself: A grade is feedback, not identity.** It shows where you are today, not who you are forever.

- **Track growth, not perfection.** Instead of asking, "Did I get an A?" ask, "Did I understand more than I did last week?"

- **Normalize mistakes.** Every single person gets things wrong. It's how we learn, not a reflection of your value.

In-the-Moment Test Strategies

Even with preparation and positive thinking, the anxiety can still creep in the moment the test starts. Your heart might pound, your hands might sweat, and your brain might start shouting, "I can't do this." The good news? There are ways to calm your body and refocus your mind while you're actually taking the test.

Here are proven strategies you can use in real time:

1. Start with Your Breath

Your breath is one of the fastest tools you have to send a "calm down" signal to your nervous system.

What to Try:

- **Box Breathing:** Before you read any questions, do a round of box breathing. This settles your body and helps you think more clearly.

- **Anchor Breath:** Quietly say to yourself on the inhale, "I am," and on the exhale, "okay." Even just one minute of this can reduce racing thoughts.

- **Micro-breaks:** If your anxiety rises again during the test, pause for a breath or two between sections. It's not wasted time, it's time that helps you think better.

2. Manage the Panic Spiral

When your brain freezes or spirals into "what if" thoughts, it needs direction, not judgment.

What to Try:

- **Name what's happening:** Silently say, "This is anxiety, not danger." Naming it separates you from it.

- **Ground yourself:** Press your feet into the floor. Notice five things you see, four things you feel, three things you hear. Come back to the room.

- **Shift your self-talk:** Instead of "I can't do this," try "One question at a time," or "I've done hard things before."

3. Tackle the Easy Questions First

Starting with questions you know builds momentum and boosts confidence.

What to Try:

- **Scan and mark:** On your first pass, mark the hard questions and skip them. Come back once you've answered the ones you're sure of.

- **Stack small wins:** Each correct answer reinforces the message to your brain that you *can* do this.

- **Use positive pacing:** Don't race, but don't linger either. If you feel stuck, move on and come back later.

4. Use Visual Grounding

Key Insight: Sometimes all it takes is something physical to bring your brain back from the edge of panic.

What to Try:

- **Bring a calming object:** A smooth stone, a fidget item, or a comforting bracelet, just something to touch or see can calm your nervous system.

- **Draw a star or smiley on your test:** It's a reminder that this is just a test, it's not life or death.

- **Glance at a mantra:** If your teacher allows it, keep a sticky note on your desk that says, "One step at a time," or "You've got this."

5. Know Your "Reset" Move

Create a tiny personal ritual to help you reset anytime panic sneaks in.

What to Try:

- **Touch your fingertips together.** It's discreet and brings your attention back to your body.

- **Count slowly to five.** Not fast. Slowly. One number for each breath.

- **Stretch your hands or roll your shoulders.** Just enough movement to interrupt the anxious energy.

These in-the-moment tools are like mental first aid. They may not eliminate anxiety completely, but they help you *function through it* and that's often the most powerful win of all.

Homework Overload

Time Management Basics

When everything feels urgent, nothing gets done. Use a planner, set timers, and block out time for specific tasks. Prioritize the most important assignments first and don't forget to build in breaks.

Prioritizing Tasks

Ask yourself: What's due first? What takes the most energy? What can wait? These questions help you build a plan and avoid last-minute panic.

Setting Realistic Goals

Instead of chasing perfection, focus on what you can control. Break big goals into smaller, doable steps. Celebrate small wins along the way. A realistic goal isn't about impressing others, it's about helping you move forward with confidence.

Create a Study Routine

Routine brings structure. Build in predictable times to study and rest. Keep it flexible, but consistent enough that your brain starts to trust the process.

Creating Boundaries

Separating School from Home Life

When school takes over your evenings, weekends, and even your dreams, it's time to create space. Keep schoolwork out of your bed. Set a clear "stop" time in the evening.

Protecting Your Downtime

Rest is not earned it's essential. Block out time that's just for you: walks, music, creativity, or just doing nothing without guilt.

Scheduling "Non-School" Fun

Joy is a protective factor against anxiety. Schedule social time, hobbies, or activities that remind you who you are outside of school.

Managing Extracurriculars

Choosing What Matters Most

In high school, it often feels like you're building a resume for your future: college applications, internships, scholarship essays.

Everywhere you look, there's pressure to be impressive. Join all the clubs. Lead every group. Volunteer on weekends. Take the hardest classes. The problem? When everything matters, nothing truly does. It's okay to not do everything.

In fact, doing *less* with more intention is often the healthier, more impactful path. When your schedule is packed with obligations that don't light you up, your energy drains fast. You start running on autopilot, checking off boxes while losing touch with what actually makes you feel alive.

So how do you choose what matters most?

Start by getting honest about what fuels you and what doesn't. Think about the activities, people, or classes that leave you feeling energized, not exhausted. Which ones spark curiosity or joy? Which ones make you forget to check the clock? These are your clues.

On the flip side, take note of the things that feel heavy. The ones you dread. The ones you signed up for because you thought you "should," not because you wanted to. Sometimes we stay in these things out of guilt or fear of missing out, fear of disappointing others, fear of seeming like a quitter. But here's the truth: your time and energy are not unlimited. Every "yes" you give is a "no" to something else, often to rest, creativity, or emotional well-being.

Choosing what matters most doesn't mean giving up on goals or responsibilities. It means aligning your time with your values. It's the difference between joining a dozen clubs to impress someone else, and committing to one or two that genuinely matter to *you* because they reflect your interests, your strengths, or your dreams.

This process takes courage. It means stepping back from the noise and saying, "What's truly important to *me* right now?" Your answer might change over time, and that's okay. You don't have to stick with something forever just because you started it. Growth means outgrowing things.

A helpful strategy is to list all your current commitments and rate them in two ways:

1. How much energy they give you, and

2. how aligned they are with your long-term values or goals.

If something scores low in both, it may be time to step away. Letting go of one thing can open space for something better or simply for rest.

You're allowed to make decisions based on *what matters to you* not just what looks good on paper or makes other people proud. That kind of alignment builds real confidence, the kind that lasts beyond high school or college applications. In the end, success isn't about how much you did. It's about how fully you showed up for the things that mattered most.

Saying "No" with Confidence

Saying "no" might be one of the hardest things you learn to do as a teen but it's also one of the most powerful.

When you're juggling school, friendships, extracurriculars, family expectations, and your own mental health, your time and energy become two of your most valuable resources. Yet, it's easy to give them away often out of guilt, pressure, or fear of missing out. You say yes because you don't want to disappoint someone. You agree to help even when you're already stretched too thin. You sign up for something that makes you anxious because you're afraid of what others might think if you don't.

Key Insight:

"No" is a complete sentence.

You don't owe anyone a lengthy explanation or a perfectly worded excuse to protect your own well-being. Boundaries are a form of self-respect, and saying no is one of the most practical ways to set those boundaries. Still, it takes practice.

Let's start with the fear: You might worry that saying no makes you selfish, unreliable, or rude. But being honest about your limits isn't rude, it's responsible. When you say yes to everything, you eventually burn out, and then you can't show up fully for anything. Saying no allows you to say yes to what truly matters.

You also don't have to wait until you're on the verge of collapse to say it. You can say no early, clearly, and kindly. Here are some examples that work in real life:

- "Thanks for asking, but I'm not able to help with that right now."

- "I really appreciate the invite, but I need a quiet night tonight."

- "That sounds great, but I'm already committed to something else."

These responses are respectful, direct, and don't leave much room for guilt-tripping. You don't need to overexplain or apologize excessively. In fact, over-apologizing can make you feel like you've done something wrong when you haven't.

If someone tries to push back or pressure you into changing your mind, that's a red flag not a reflection on your decision. A true friend or supportive adult will respect your boundaries, even if they're disappointed. You're not responsible for managing other people's emotions. You *are* responsible for managing your own.

And don't forget: saying no doesn't just protect your time. It protects your mental space. Anxiety thrives when we feel overcommitted, overwhelmed, and like we've lost control of our own schedule. Each time you say no with intention, you're choosing peace over pressure. You're choosing yourself.

Saying no also builds confidence. The more you do it, the easier it becomes. You'll stop second-guessing your instincts. You'll start trusting your inner compass. That's a life skill that will serve you far beyond your teenage years.

Remember: you're allowed to choose rest. You're allowed to choose what works for you. And you're allowed to say no even to good things if they're not the *right* things for you right now.

Weekend Reboot Plans: Using Rest to Recharge

Weekends often come with a false promise: the idea that they'll be restful, relaxing, and completely yours. But for many teens, weekends get packed with homework, chores, catch-up tasks, and sometimes even more pressure than weekdays. Instead of being a break, they become a blur, leaving you just as tired on Monday morning as you were on Friday afternoon.

That's where the concept of a **weekend reboot** comes in. This isn't about being lazy or wasting time, it's about being intentional with your rest. Think of it as recharging your battery, mentally and physically, so you're not running on empty by the time the new week starts.

The first step in a weekend reboot is permission. You have to give yourself permission to slow down. In a world that praises busyness, choosing rest can feel wrong, even selfish. But real productivity requires recovery. Just like muscles need rest to grow stronger, your brain needs downtime to process and reset.

So, what does that actually look like?

It might mean sleeping in without feeling guilty about it. Sleep isn't laziness it's one of the most important tools you have to support your mood, memory, focus, and resilience. Aim to get extra rest if your body is asking for it.

It might mean **eating breakfast slowly** without rushing out the door. Savor the food. Take your time. Let your nervous system know you're safe and unhurried. Slowing down your mornings can change the tone of your entire day.

It might mean **doing one thing you love**, just because. Watch a show you've been meaning to catch up on. Paint, draw, or journal.

Bake something new. Go outside and feel the sun on your skin. You don't need a productivity goal to enjoy yourself. Joy is a goal in itself.

It also helps to create **a soft structure** for your weekend. You don't need to plan every hour, but you can block out chunks of time for specific needs: one hour for rest, two for homework, one for fun, another for prepping for the week ahead. This keeps your weekend from slipping away but still gives you freedom.

One powerful habit to build into your weekend reboot is a **Sunday night reset**. This could be a calming routine that signals to your brain: "We're preparing for a new start." It might include tidying up your room, making a to-do list for the week, laying out your clothes, or journaling about how last week went. It's not about perfection it's about transition.

The most important part: **Rest is productive**. It's an investment in your mental health, your academic success, and your ability to show up fully in your life. If you keep running without stopping, anxiety finds more space to grow. But when you pause intentionally, regularly you give your mind the care it needs to function at its best.

Key Insight:

Your weekend doesn't need to be packed to be meaningful. Sometimes, the most powerful thing you can do is step back, breathe, and reboot.

Reflection Questions

- What part of school causes you the most stress and why?

- How do you usually react when you feel overwhelmed?

- What support or change would help your school experience feel more manageable?

Action Step

Choose one academic habit to shift this week whether that's starting homework earlier, asking a question in class, or taking a break when you need one. Write it down. Track how it goes.

Even one change can reduce school anxiety and build confidence.

CHAPTER 7

SOCIAL STRESS & FITTING IN

Fitting in can feel like a full-time job in your teen years. Whether it's navigating friend groups, unspoken rules of texting, or how you show up in group chats, the social world can be overwhelming. If anxiety follows you into classrooms, hallways, and even your DMs, this chapter is for you.

Understanding Social Anxiety

Social anxiety isn't just shyness. It's a deep fear of being judged, rejected, or humiliated in social settings, even ones that seem casual to others.

Common thoughts:

- "What if I say something weird?"
- "Everyone's staring at me."
- "They're probably thinking I don't belong."

Key Insight:

Social anxiety thrives on imagined judgment. What you think people are thinking about you is usually much harsher than the truth.

What Triggers Social Stress

1. Group Situations: Group projects, lunch tables, and parties can make you feel exposed.

2. Performance Settings: Presentations, reading aloud, or answering in class may trigger panic.

3. Digital Spaces: Group chats, social media comments, or being left on "read" can create anxiety.

The Inner Critic in Public

Social stress is often made worse by the voice in your head that says:

- "They don't actually like you."

- "You're being annoying."

- "You're so awkward."

Recognizing and challenging these thoughts is the first step toward peace.

Friendship Struggles

Friendships are important, but they're also one of the biggest sources of stress for teens.

Feeling Left Out:

- It stings when you're not invited or when a group makes inside jokes without you.

- Social media makes this worse by showing you what you missed.

Toxic Dynamics:

- Do they put you down, even as a "joke"?

- Do they make you anxious more than supported?

Healthy friendships include respect, mutual effort, and room for your emotions.

Navigating Conflict:

- You can stand up for yourself calmly: "I didn't like how that felt."

- Not every disagreement means a friendship is over.

- If someone keeps hurting you and won't change, it's okay to walk away.

"Everyone Else is Fine"

When you're scrolling through social media or walking the school hallways, it can feel like everyone else has it together. Smiling selfies, perfect outfits, straight-A report cards, big friend groups. It all paints a picture of lives that look happy, confident, and calm. Meanwhile, you might be battling racing thoughts, sleepless nights, or a tight chest every time someone asks how you're doing. It's easy to think, *"Why am I the only one who feels like this?"*

But here's the truth: you're not the only one. Most people don't post their struggles. They don't share the nights they cried in the shower, the panic attacks they had in their room, or the days they stayed in bed because the world felt too heavy. Social media is a highlight reel, not a behind-the-scenes documentary.

Even in real life, people learn to hide their anxiety well. You can be outgoing and still feel overwhelmed. You can get good grades and still feel like you're failing inside. You can laugh with friends and still go home and cry. Anxiety doesn't always look like someone curled up in a corner, it often looks like someone who's trying really hard to keep it all together.

The idea that "everyone else is fine" feeds a dangerous lie: that there's something wrong with you. That if you were stronger, more disciplined, or more normal, you wouldn't feel this way. That's simply not true. Anxiety affects millions of people, especially teens, and it doesn't discriminate.

It's also important to remember that comparison warps your view. You might be comparing your worst days to someone else's best moments. You're judging your inner chaos against someone else's outer calm. That's not a fair match. When you only see someone's highlight reel, you don't see the whole person. And you're not supposed to.

So, what can you do about this comparison trap?

First, practice awareness. When you find yourself thinking, *"Everyone else is doing better than me,"* pause and challenge that thought. Ask yourself: *Do I know that for sure? Or am I guessing based on what I see?*

Second, limit your exposure to unrealistic content. If certain accounts or platforms make you feel worse about yourself, take a break. Curate your feed with content that makes you feel understood, not judged.

Third, open up to people you trust. You might be surprised to learn that your friends are dealing with anxiety too, but no one's talking about it. Being honest about your experience can break the silence and create deeper connections.

Most importantly, remind yourself that your path doesn't need to match anyone else's. It's okay to have struggles. It's okay to take your time. Healing isn't a race, and you don't have to prove anything to anyone.

Social Media vs. Reality

Social media can feel like a window into everyone else's lives, but it's often more like a carefully curated stage. What you see online isn't reality. It's a filtered version of life, edited for attention, approval, and appearances. When you're already feeling anxious, comparing yourself to that version of other people can make everything worse.

You might see someone post a photo laughing with a group of friends, and suddenly you wonder why you weren't invited or why you feel so alone. You scroll past a selfie with glowing skin and think, *"Why don't I look like that?"* Or maybe someone posts their straight-A report card or acceptance letter, and now you're spiraling, questioning your own accomplishments. This kind of constant comparison doesn't just affect your mood, it can chip away at your self-worth.

What most people don't show are the messy parts. They don't share the fights they had with friends, the hours they spent crying, the nights they couldn't sleep, or the anxious thoughts they're trying to quiet. Behind every perfect-looking post could be a person struggling, just like you. But when all you see are polished, filtered snapshots, it's easy to assume everyone else is happier, more successful, or more put-together.

Even things like filters and editing apps play a role in distorting reality. A photo can be edited in seconds to smooth out skin, whiten teeth, change body shape, or add a glow that doesn't exist in real life. The final image might look effortless, but it's often anything but real. Yet, your brain still reacts to it like it's the truth.

For teens especially, this constant exposure to idealized images and experiences can increase feelings of anxiety, loneliness, and not being "enough." It creates invisible standards no one can meet, not even the people posting them. You start to believe that you're the only one struggling, when in reality, almost everyone is editing their lives before sharing them.

So, what can you do?

Start by reminding yourself that what you see online is not the full story. When you notice yourself feeling anxious or inadequate after scrolling, pause and question what you're believing. Ask yourself: *"Is this a highlight or the whole picture?"*

Consider doing a digital detox or curating your feed. Follow accounts that promote authenticity and make you feel seen rather than small. Unfollow or mute accounts that consistently make you feel worse about yourself. Your feed should support your mental health, not hurt it.

You can also make a point to be more real in your own posts. If you're comfortable, share the ups and the downs. Let your feed reflect *you* not just what you think others want to see. This can create space for more honest conversations and help others feel less alone, too.

Remember: social media is a tool, not a mirror. It doesn't define your worth, your beauty, or your progress. Reality is messier, more human, and more beautiful than any post could ever show.

Why Comparison Hurts

Comparison is something almost every teen struggles with at some point. It's natural to look at someone else's life, grades, appearance, or talents and wonder how you measure up. But what starts as a quick thought can quickly spiral into self-doubt, anxiety, and feeling like you're falling behind. That's because comparison, especially during adolescence, hits you where you're most vulnerable, your identity.

Your teen years are a time of figuring out who you are. But when you're constantly measuring yourself against others, it becomes harder to hear your own voice. You might start to believe that your value depends on being as popular as someone else, as athletic, as attractive, or as smart. Slowly, you start editing yourself what you wear, how you talk, what you like just to match a version of someone else you've decided is "better." That disconnection from your authentic self doesn't just lead to confusion; it fuels anxiety. Because deep down, you know you're living a version of someone else's life not your own.

Comparison also creates pressure. If your classmate gets a scholarship, you might feel like you're not doing enough. If your friend gets invited to every party, you might start wondering what's "wrong" with you. But the truth is, life isn't a race or a competition. Everyone has a different timeline and different strengths. What's right for someone else may not be right for you, and that's not only okay, it's *necessary*.

Another hidden danger of comparison is that it's often based on incomplete information. You don't know what someone else is going through behind the scenes. The person you admire for being confident may struggle with their own self-worth. The classmate who seems to have it all together may be facing pressure you can't see. When you compare your behind-the-scenes to someone else's highlight reel, you're playing a losing game.

Comparison also steals joy. Think about a time when you felt proud of something maybe you did well on a test, had a great performance, or just felt really good about your outfit. Then you saw someone else doing even "better," and suddenly your happiness disappeared. That's what comparison does. It robs you of the ability to celebrate your own wins because it convinces you they're not good *enough*.

To start shifting away from this trap, practice self-awareness. When you notice yourself comparing, pause and ask: *What story am I telling myself right now?* Often, it's a story that you're not enough which isn't true. Try reframing your thoughts. Instead of saying, *"I'll never be as good as them,"* try, *"I'm working on my own goals, and that's okay."*

Also, focus on your own progress. What were you struggling with a year ago that you've since improved? What strengths do you have that others may not see? Keep a list of small wins, not to show off, but to remind yourself that *you* are growing, in your own way, on your own timeline. Ultimately, the only person you need to be better than is the person you were yesterday. That's the only comparison that counts and the one that actually leads to confidence and peace.

Common Thoughts:

- "Everyone else seems more confident than me."

- "Why can they talk so easily while I freeze up?"

- "Other people always look better than I do."

Key Insights:

Comparison keeps you focused on someone else's story. Healing begins when you return your attention to your own.

CHAPTER 8

CALMING TECHNIQUES THAT ACTUALLY WORK

Anxiety can feel unpredictable. One moment you are fine, and the next your heart is racing, your thoughts are spinning, and your body feels like it is on high alert. The truth is that anxiety does not begin in your mind alone. It is a full body experience. This is why calming techniques are not about forcing yourself to "think positive" but about learning how to signal safety to your nervous system.

This chapter gives you practical, simple tools that work in real moments. They will not eliminate anxiety forever, but they can interrupt the spiral, settle your body, and give you back control when things feel intense.

Why Calming Techniques Matter

When your nervous system is activated, your thinking brain becomes less available. You cannot reason with yourself effectively when your body is still sounding the alarm. Calming techniques work because they do the opposite. They quiet the alarm so your brain can return to clarity, problem solving, and emotional balance.

Calming your body is not avoidance. It is preparation. You are creating the internal conditions you need in order to move forward.

1. Breathing That Calms the Body

Breathing is one of the fastest ways to shift your emotional state. Anxiety pushes your breath higher into your chest, which tells your brain to stay alert. Deep and slow breathing sends the opposite message.

Technique 1: Belly Breathing

How to practice:

1. Sit or stand comfortably.

2. Place one hand on your stomach.

3. Inhale slowly through your nose and let your belly rise.

4. Exhale gently through your mouth.

Why it works:

Belly breathing activates your parasympathetic nervous system. This is the part of your body responsible for calming, rest, and recovery. Even a few slow breaths can change how your body feels.

Technique 2: Four Count Breathing

Inhale for four counts

Hold for four counts

Exhale for four counts

Hold for four counts

Repeat for a few rounds

Why it works:

When you count, you interrupt anxious thoughts. When you slow your exhale, your heart rate decreases automatically.

Technique 3: Extended Exhale

Inhale for a count of four

Exhale for a count of six

Why it works:

A longer exhale naturally lowers tension in the body, which is especially helpful during panic or overwhelm.

2. Grounding Techniques for Racing Thoughts

When anxiety takes over, thoughts can feel loud, chaotic, and fast. Grounding helps bring your attention back to the present moment.

Technique 1: Five Senses Reset

Name:

- Five things you can see

- Four things you can touch

- Three things you can hear

- Two things you can smell

- One thing you can taste

Why it works:

Your brain cannot stay fully in the future or the past while observing your senses. This breaks the cycle of worry.

Technique 2: Object Focus

Hold something small like a bracelet, key, or rock. Notice its texture, color, weight, and temperature.

Why it works:

Focusing on one physical object redirects your mind and gives your nervous system a point of stability.

Technique 3: Orientation Technique

Turn your head slowly and look at the objects around you. Name where you are, the date, and what time of day it is.

Why it works:

This communicates to your brain that you are not in danger. You are grounding yourself in real time.

3. Calming Through Movement

Anxiety prepares your body to act. Movement gives that energy somewhere to go.

Technique 1: Gentle Walking

A five minute walk can release tension, settle your breath, and clear your thoughts.

Technique 2: Stretching the Upper Body

Shoulder rolls

Neck stretches

Slow arm circles

Why it works:

These exercises relax areas that hold stress. When your muscles soften, your mind often follows.

Technique 3: Shake It Out

Shake your arms, legs, and hands for ten to fifteen seconds.

Why it works:

This is a natural way to release stored adrenaline. Many animals shake after a stressful event and humans can benefit from the same instinct.

4. Releasing Mental Pressure

Anxiety thrives in silence. When your mind holds too much, small things start to feel bigger.

Technique 1: Brain Dump

Set a timer for three minutes. Write down every thought in your mind without editing.

Why it works:

Putting thoughts on paper reduces the pressure to hold everything in your head. It creates space and clarity.

Technique 2: Naming the Feeling

Say to yourself:

"I am feeling anxious."

"I am feeling overwhelmed."

Why it works:

Naming a feeling activates the thinking part of your brain. This makes the emotion feel more manageable.

Technique 3: Calm Statements

Examples:

"I am safe in this moment."

"This feeling will pass."

"I know how to support myself."

Why it works:

Simple statements cue your nervous system to step out of panic mode.

5. Tools for Panic Moments

Panic can feel sudden and powerful. These techniques help you regain control quickly.

Technique 1: Temperature Change

Hold something cold, place a cool cloth on your face, or take a sip of cold water.

Why it works:

A quick temperature shift triggers the body's natural calming reflex.

Technique 2: Anchor Points

Place your feet firmly on the floor and your hands on a table or your legs. Apply gentle pressure.

Why it works:

Physical grounding brings you back into your body when panic creates a sense of drifting or detachment.

Technique 3: Slowing Your Exhale

Panic shortens your breath. Extending your exhale interrupts this pattern and lowers your heart rate.

Reflection Questions

1. Which calming techniques feel most natural to you?
2. When does your anxiety tend to show up in your body?
3. Which technique will you practice regularly so it becomes easier to use during hard moments?

Action Step

Pick one calming technique from this chapter and practice it once a day for the next week. You do not need to wait for anxiety to practice. The more familiar the tool becomes, the easier it is to use when you really need it.

Journaling Your Thoughts:

- Brain dump: Get all the anxious thoughts out on paper

- Focused journaling: Write about one situation and explore the thoughts, feelings, and facts.

- Prompts: "What am I feeling right now?" or "What do I need most today?"

Meditation for Teens:

- Use an app or YouTube video

- Try body scan meditations or guided breathing

- Start with 3–5 minutes and build from there

Creative & Physical Outlets

Key Insight: Movement and creativity help release anxiety that gets stuck in your body.

Music Therapy:

- Create calming playlists

- Use music to shift your mood

- Play an instrument or sing to express emotion

Movement for the Mind:

- Try yoga poses like Child's Pose or Forward Fold

- Go for a walk or dance it out

- Join a sport you enjoy

Art for Expression:

- Doodle your feelings

- Color mandalas or abstract shapes

- Draw what anxiety feels like to externalize it

Creating a Calm Environment

Your space can affect your state of mind.

- Use soft lighting

- Keep one corner clean and cozy

- Use scents like lavender or eucalyptus

Building Habits for Long-Term Calm

Key Insight:

You'll feel the most benefit when you make calming tools part of your routine not just when you're already overwhelmed.

- Start or end your day with one calming practice

- Keep a "calm kit" with items that soothe you

- Schedule moments of quiet, even for 5 minutes

Reflection Questions:

1. Which calming technique feels easiest to try today?

2. What usually works best for you when anxiety hits?

3. Where could you build more calm into your daily routine?

Action Step:

Create your personal "Calm Plan." List 3 techniques you can use during anxiety, 2 tools to keep in your bag or locker, and 1 calming activity to build into your routine each day.

CHAPTER 9

WHAT IS CBT (COGNITIVE BEHAVIORAL THERAPY)?

Cognitive Behavioral Therapy known as CBT, is one of the most researched and effective tools for managing anxiety, especially in teens. It is widely used by therapists, school counselors, and mental health professionals because it teaches practical skills that you can use in everyday life. CBT is not about analyzing your past or digging through childhood memories. It is about understanding the patterns in your thoughts, emotions, and actions right now, and learning how to shift them in healthier directions.

This chapter breaks down what CBT is, why it works, and how you can start using its techniques in your own life.

What Is CBT?

CBT, or Cognitive Behavioral Therapy, is one of the most effective and widely used tools for managing anxiety. It's not about lying on a couch while someone analyzes your childhood. Instead, it's a practical, hands-on approach that helps you understand how your thoughts, feelings, and actions are all connected and how changing one can influence the others in powerful ways.

Let's say you have a big presentation coming up at school. You think, *"I'm going to mess this up."* That thought makes you feel nervous and panicky. Because you feel anxious, you avoid preparing or decide to skip school that day. The result? Your fear is reinforced. Your brain now believes that the only way to escape that scary feeling is to avoid the situation. The next time something similar comes up, your anxiety may hit even harder.

CBT helps break that cycle.

It starts with **awareness**. CBT teaches you how to notice the thoughts running through your mind especially the negative or distorted ones. These might include:

- *"I'm going to fail."*

- *"Everyone will laugh at me."*

- *"If I don't do this perfectly, I'm worthless."*

These are called **cognitive distortions** unhelpful thought patterns that trick you into seeing things in a more negative light than they really are. CBT doesn't just tell you to "think positively." It shows you how to **question those thoughts**, test them against facts, and replace them with more balanced thinking.

For example, instead of *"I'm going to fail,"* a more realistic thought might be, *"I'm nervous, but I've prepared. I can do my best."* This shift in thinking leads to less anxiety and more confidence. You may still feel nervous, but that nervousness no longer controls your behavior.

CBT also teaches **behavioral strategies** the "B" part of the therapy. These are tools to help you face fears, rather than avoid them. One common CBT tool is **exposure**, where you slowly and safely face the things you're afraid of, in small steps. So, if you're afraid of speaking up in class, you might start by answering a yes/no question, then work your way up to sharing a full opinion. Each small success builds your confidence and teaches your brain: *Hey, I survived that. It wasn't as bad as I thought.*

Another important aspect of CBT is learning how to **track your progress**. You might use a journal or worksheet to write down your anxious thoughts, what triggered them, and what you did in response.

Over time, you start to see patterns and more importantly, improvements. You begin to notice that certain thoughts aren't true, that you're more resilient than you gave yourself credit for, and that change is possible.

CBT can be done with a licensed therapist, but many of the tools are also available in workbooks, apps, and self-help guides. In this book, we'll cover several CBT-based exercises you can use on your own to understand your anxiety and respond to it differently.

The heart of CBT is this: **You're not stuck.** Even if your anxiety feels overwhelming, there are tools and thought shifts that can help. You have the power to change your story one thought, one action, one day at a time.

The Basic Idea:

- Your thoughts influence how you feel.

- How you feel influences what you do.

- What you do either makes things better or keeps the anxiety loop going.

Key Insight:

You don't have to believe every anxious thought. CBT gives you the tools to challenge and change them.

Why CBT Works

CBT is all about practice not perfection. It teaches you to become more aware of what's happening in your mind, so you can interrupt unhelpful cycles.

It works because:

- It's structured and focused

- You learn to spot patterns early

- You develop long-term coping skills

Identifying Unhelpful Thoughts

CBT teaches you to spot automatic thoughts, those instant reactions in your brain that often go unnoticed.

Common examples:

- "I'm going to mess this up."

- "Everyone thinks I'm weird."

- "I can't handle this."

Cognitive Distortions:

These are thought traps that fuel anxiety. Here are a few common ones:

1. Catastrophizing – expecting the worst

2. Mind reading – assuming others are judging you

3. All-or-nothing thinking – "If it's not perfect, I failed."

4. Personalizing: taking responsibility for things that were not actually your fault.

5. Overgeneralizing: turning one bad moment into a sweeping conclusion

Challenge the Thought

Once you identify an anxious thought, you can practice questioning it.

Ask yourself:

- Is this thought 100% true?

- What's the evidence for and against it?

- What would I tell a friend who had this same thought?

Try a "reframe": A reframe does not deny the feeling. It just shifts the lens.

Examples:

Thought: "I am going to fail."

Reframe: "I feel nervous, but I have prepared. I can do my best."

Thought: "Everyone thinks I am weird."

Reframe: "I cannot know what everyone thinks. People are usually focused on themselves."

Thought: "If it is not perfect, it does not count."

Reframe: "Progress matters more than perfection. Doing something imperfectly still helps me grow."

The goal is not forced positivity. The goal is balance.

Thought Log Exercise:

CBT often uses structured tools to help you practice.

Write down:

1. **Situation:** What happened?

2. **Thought:** What ran through your mind?

3. **Feeling:** How did it make you feel?

4. **Alternative Thought:** What's a more balanced way to look at this?

Behavioral Tools: Changing What You Do

CBT also focuses on behavior. Anxiety often tells you to avoid things that feel scary. Avoidance brings temporary relief, but it teaches your brain that the situation is truly dangerous, which makes anxiety stronger over time.

Behavioral tools give your brain new experiences that prove you can handle more than you think

Example:

- Thought: "If I raise my hand, I'll say something dumb."

- Experiment: Try raising your hand once in a low-stakes class.

- Outcome: Most likely, nothing bad happens and you gain confidence.

You learn through doing. The more you face fear with small actions, the less control anxiety has.

The Role of Habits

CBT also focuses on behaviors that either help or hurt your progress.

Helpful CBT Habits:

- Keeping a thought journal

- Practicing reframing daily

- Scheduling calming activities

- Facing small fears regularly

Key Insight:

Avoidance is a habit too, one that strengthens anxiety. CBT encourages you to face challenges gradually and with support.

When to Get Help with CBT

Although many CBT tools can be used on your own, there are times when working with a trained therapist is helpful. A therapist can:

- Help you understand deeper thought patterns

- Guide you through exposure steps safely

- Offer support during difficult periods

- Teach advanced CBT strategies

You may benefit from support if anxiety is:

- Interfering with school

- Affecting your relationships

- Keeping you from activities you enjoy

- Causing panic symptoms

- Making it hard to get through daily routines

CBT is a skill, and like any skill, it can grow with guidance.

Reflection Questions:

1. What anxious thoughts come up for you often?

2. Can you identify any cognitive distortions you tend to fall into?

3. What's one situation where you could try a CBT reframe this week?

Action Step:

Start a "Thought Tracker" journal for one week. Write down one anxious thought per day, and practice reframing it using questions from this chapter. Notice any patterns and what changes over time.

CHAPTER 10

WHAT IS MINDFULNESS?

Mindfulness might sound like a buzzword, but it's one of the most powerful tools you can use to manage anxiety. It's about being fully present in the moment without judgment, distraction, or pressure. In a world that constantly pulls your attention in a hundred directions, mindfulness helps you return back to yourself.

What Is Mindfulness?

Mindfulness is the practice of being fully present in the moment on purpose and without judgment. It's not about "clearing your mind" or ignoring your feelings. In fact, it's the opposite. Mindfulness teaches you to notice what's happening right now, both inside and around you, with curiosity and kindness.

Imagine your mind as a snow globe. When you're anxious, it feels like someone has shaken it up. Thoughts swirl, emotions race, and it's hard to see clearly.

Mindfulness is the act of letting the snow settle. It doesn't fix everything instantly, but it helps you see your situation more calmly, without getting lost in the storm.

At its core, mindfulness helps you build awareness. That means learning to notice what's going on in your body, like a racing heart or tight chest, your thoughts, "I can't handle this", and your emotions, like fear or frustration. Instead of trying to push those things away or fix them immediately, mindfulness invites you to observe them without reacting right away.

Why is this so powerful for anxiety? Because anxiety lives in the future. It's the, what if? voice, that spins stories about what could go wrong. Mindfulness pulls you out of those future fears and anchors you in the present moment. In this moment right here, right now you're safe. You're breathing. You're okay.

Practicing mindfulness can be as simple as:

- Focusing on your breath for 60 seconds.

- Noticing the way your feet feel on the floor.

- Observing the taste and texture of your food while eating.

- Listening to sounds around you without labeling them.

- Noticing a thought and gently letting it pass, like a cloud in the sky.

It doesn't have to be formal meditation (though that helps, too). You can bring mindfulness into everyday moments while brushing your teeth, walking to school, or even washing your hands. The goal is to slow down, check in, and return to your center.

Mindfulness also helps you respond, rather than react. Let's say someone says something that annoys you, and your first impulse is to snap back. With mindfulness, you learn to pause just for a breath and choose how to act. That tiny space between stimulus and response is where your power lies. Over time, that pause becomes easier to find.

Research shows that regular mindfulness practice can lower anxiety, reduce stress, improve focus, and even supports better sleep. It trains your brain to be more resilient, less reactive, and more present. You won't be perfect at mindfulness right away and that's okay. Your mind will wander. You'll forget to check in. Every time you come back to the present moment, you're building strength. You're teaching your brain: "I don't have to chase every worry. I can be here, now."

Mindfulness is not a magic solution. But it's one of the most accessible, stable and reliable tools you have. You can practice it anywhere, the more you do, the more it becomes a steady anchor in the waves of anxiety.

It's not about having a blank mind or being perfectly calm. It's about noticing what's happening in your body and thoughts without reacting automatically or judging yourself.

Key Insight:

Anxiety pulls you into "what if." Mindfulness brings you back to "what is."

Everyday Mindfulness Practices

You don't need a meditation cushion or hours of silence to be mindful. It's something you can practice anytime, anywhere.

Here are some ways to build it into your day:

Mindful Eating:

- Focus on the smell, taste, and texture of your food.
- Eat slowly, without distractions like your phone.
- Notice how your body feels before and after eating.

Mindful Walking:

- Walk slower than usual and notice each step.
- Feel your feet connect with the ground.
- Listen to the sounds around you.

Mindful Listening:

- When someone's talking, give your full attention.
- Don't plan what to say next just listen.
- Notice how it changes the conversation.

How Mindfulness Helps Anxiety

When your mind races with fear, judgment, or future-thinking, mindfulness brings you back to the now. It's like hitting a mental reset button.

Benefits of mindfulness include:

- Slowing down anxious thoughts

- Reducing physical tension

- Helping you respond calmly instead of reacting impulsively

It also builds awareness. The more you notice your patterns, the easier it is to shift them.

Mindfulness for Difficult Emotions

RAIN Technique:

1. Recognize what you're feeling (e.g., fear, anger, shame)

2. Allow it to be there without pushing it away

3. Investigate gently: "Where do I feel this in my body?"

4. Nurture yourself: "What do I need right now?"

This helps you sit with big emotions without being overwhelmed by them.

Meditation for Beginners

Meditation is a form of mindfulness where you intentionally set aside time to be still and observe.

Simple Breathing Meditation:

- Sit or lie down comfortably

- Close your eyes and focus on your breath

- Inhale and exhale slowly

- If your mind wanders (and it will), gently bring it back

Start with just 2–3 minutes. Use a timer or an app if it helps.

You can also try:

- Body scan meditations
- Loving-kindness meditations (sending kindness to yourself and others)
- Guided meditations on YouTube or apps

Key Insight:

Meditation isn't about stopping thoughts it's about learning to not follow them.

Creating a Mindful Space

You can build a small sanctuary wherever you are. A few suggestions:

- Keep a mindfulness journal
- Light a calming candle
- Use noise-canceling headphones or soft music
- Have an object (like a stone or piece of fabric) to hold when you need grounding

Mindfulness in School and Social Settings

Even in noisy or busy places, mindfulness can help:

- Before a test: Take 3 deep breaths and notice your feet on the floor
- In a conversation: Focus on the speaker's words and your breathing
- During lunch: Savor your food instead of scrolling through your phone

Reflection Questions:

1. What does be "present" mean to you?

2. When do you find yourself most distracted or anxious?

3. What's one small way you can build mindfulness into your routine?

Action Step:

Choose one mindfulness practice from this chapter to try each day for the next week. Keep a short journal of what you notice physically, mentally, and emotionally. You might be surprised by the impact of just a few mindful minutes.

CHAPTER 11

CHANGING YOUR THOUGHTS

One of the most powerful tools for managing anxiety is learning how to change your thoughts. Your thoughts create your emotions, which then influence your behaviors. When your inner dialogue is full of fear, self-doubt, or negativity, it becomes difficult to feel calm and confident. But here's the good news, you can train your mind to think differently.

How Thoughts Fuel Anxiety

An anxious mind often jumps to worst-case scenarios. It misinterprets neutral situations as threats and spirals into "what if" thinking.

Examples of anxious thought patterns:

- "They didn't text back, so they must hate me."

- "If I don't do this perfectly, I'll fail."

These thoughts may feel automatic, but they're not permanent. When you begin noticing them, you can choose new ways to respond.

Types of Unhelpful Thoughts

Cognitive distortions are the mental traps that fuel anxiety. Here are some of the most common ones:

1. Catastrophizing – Expecting disaster ("If I fail this quiz, I'll ruin my future.")

2. Black-and-White Thinking – Seeing things as all good or all bad ("If I'm not the best, I'm worthless.")

3. Mind Reading – Assuming you know what others are thinking ("They must think I'm weird.")

4. Overgeneralizing – Using one event to predict everything ("This one bad day means my whole week will be bad.")

5. Filtering – Ignoring the positives and focusing only on the negatives

Key Insight:

You don't have to believe everything you think. Just because a thought pops up doesn't mean it's true or helpful.

Reframing Your Thoughts

Once you notice an anxious thought, the next step is to challenge it. Ask yourself:

- Is this thought based on facts or fear?

- What would I tell a friend who thought this?

- What's a more balanced way to look at this?

Practice:

- Thought: "I'll never be good at this."

- Reframe: "I'm still learning, and progress takes time."

- Thought: "They're probably laughing at me."

- Reframe: "I don't have evidence for that. They might just be busy."

Building Thought Awareness:

Try these exercises to become more aware of your thoughts:

1. Mindful Check-I – Set a timer for 3 minutes and notice what

2. thoughts come up without judging them.

3. Name Your Narrator – Give your anxious voice a name (e.g., "Worry Wanda") to help separate it from your identity.

4. Thought Replacement Chart– Create two columns: one for anxious thoughts and one for reframes. Add to it regularly.

Key Insight:

You are not your thoughts you're the observer of your thoughts. This awareness gives you the power to choose.

When Thought Patterns Are Stubborn

Some thought loops are deeply ingrained and may take longer to shift. That's okay.

Tips for tough patterns:

- Talk to a counselor or therapist for support

- Pair thought work with calming techniques like breathing or movement

- Celebrate small wins ("I noticed the thought, progress!")

You don't need to erase anxiety to make progress. You just need to create enough space between the thought and the reaction.

Reflection Questions:

1. What are 2–3 anxious thoughts you often notice?

2. Which cognitive distortion do you relate to most?

3. What's one affirmation you can begin using today?

Action Step:

Start a Thought Reframing Journal. Each day, write down one anxious thought and practice reframing it. Over time, this journal will become evidence of your growth and a reminder of your power to shift your mindset.

CHAPTER 12

MANAGING THE INNER CRITIC

Inside every anxious teen is an inner voice that whispers doubts, criticizes choices, and fuels fear. This voice, often called the inner critic, can feel loud and convincing. Learning how to recognize and manage this voice is a powerful way to reduce anxiety and increase confidence.

What Is the Inner Critic?

The inner critic is the part of your mind that tells you:

- "You're not good enough."

- "Everyone's judging you."

- "You always mess things up."

It often shows up in moments of pressure, uncertainty or comparison. Although it sometimes tries to protect you from embarrassment or failure, it often limits you instead.

Key Insight:

The inner critic isn't truth, it's a thought habit and like any habit, it can be changed.

Why Your Brain Believes It

Your brain is wired for survival, not happiness. That means it focuses on potential threats even imagined ones. The inner critic develops from:

- Childhood experiences or harsh feedback

- Fear of rejection or not fitting in

- A desire to avoid failure at all costs

When your brain hears the same negative messages over and over, it starts to believe them. That's why it's so important to introduce a new voice one of kindness, truth, and support.

Challenging the Thought

Step one in managing your inner critic is identifying when it's speaking. Common signs include:

- Feeling suddenly discouraged or ashamed

- Feeling afraid to try something new

- Speaking to yourself more harshly than you would a friend

How to challenge it:

1. Catch the Thought: "I always screw this up."

2. Question It: "Is that really true? Always?"

3. Reframe It: "I've struggled with this before, but I'm learning."

The more you practice this, the easier it becomes to separate your real self from the anxious voice in your head.

Practicing Self-Compassion

Self-compassion means treating yourself with the same kindness you'd offer others. It's not about making excuses, it's about acknowledging your struggles without adding shame.

Ways to practice:

- Speak to yourself as you would to a friend: "It's okay to be learning."

- Write a compassionate letter to yourself when you feel down

- Remember that imperfection is part of being human

Key Insight:

Self-compassion doesn't make you soft. It makes you strong enough to grow through hard things.

Daily Affirmations to Rewire Self-Talk

Affirmations are short, powerful statements you can repeat to yourself to challenge negative thoughts and shift your mindset. Think of them as mental nutrition fuel for your confidence and emotional well-being. When repeated regularly, affirmations help rewire the brain and create a more supportive inner voice.

Why Affirmations Work

Our brain is wired to believe what it hears most often. If you constantly hear yourself saying things like "I'm not good enough," that message becomes your inner truth. But the reverse is also true, when you feed your brain positive, empowering thoughts, it begins to shift how you view yourself and your world.

Affirmations work best when they are:

- Believable: They should feel possible, even if they stretch you.

- Present tense: Speak as if the change is happening now.

- Personal: Use "I" statements that reflect your needs and identity.

How to Use Affirmations

- Say them aloud in the mirror each morning.

- Write them in your journal.

- Set reminders on your phone to repeat them throughout the day.

- Pair them with deep breaths or calming music.

The goal is consistency, not perfection. You don't have to believe them fully right away just practice showing up for yourself.

Examples of Daily Affirmations

Here are affirmations to help rewire negative self-talk, grouped by themes:

For Self-Worth:

- I am enough exactly as I am.
- My worth isn't based on my productivity.
- I don't need to earn love or acceptance.

For Calm and Anxiety Relief:

- I am safe in this moment.
- I can handle what comes my way.
- My breath brings me calm.

For Confidence:

- I trust myself.
- I am proud of how far I've come.
- I have everything I need to move forward.

For Resilience:

- I've survived hard things before, and I will again.
- My challenges help me grow.
- I am rebuilding one step at a time.

For Letting Go:

- I release what no longer serves me.
- I don't need to hold on to every thought.
- It's okay to not have all the answers.

For Connection and Belonging:

- I am not alone.

- I deserve care and support.

- I am allowed to take up space.

Creating Your Own Affirmations

If you want to make your own affirmations:

1. Identify a negative belief you often repeat.

2. Flip it into a compassionate truth.

3. Make it specific and in the present tense.

Example:

- Negative belief: "I always mess things up."

- Affirmation: "I am learning and growing with each experience."

Final Note

Affirmations are a powerful tool in your healing journey. Each time you say something kind to yourself, you're rewriting the story. You're choosing hope over fear, growth over perfection, and compassion over criticism. Speak gently. You're listening.

Building Confidence Brick by Brick

Confidence doesn't mean never feeling fear. It means trusting yourself enough to act even when you're nervous. You build it through action, repetition, and patience.

Try this:

- Take one small action that scares you every week

- Celebrate tiny wins (not just big accomplishments)

- Keep a "confidence file" of things you've done that made you proud

Over time, this file becomes proof that you're stronger than the voice that says you're not.

Reflection Questions:

1. What does your inner critic usually say?

2. When did you first notice this voice?

3. What's one new belief you want to start practicing?

Action Step:

Start a "Compassion Challenge" for one week. Each day, write down one thing you criticized yourself for and rewrite it with compassion. At the end of the week, notice how it shifts your mindset and mood.

CHAPTER 13

WHEN THINGS FEEL TOO HEAVY

Sometimes anxiety doesn't just feel like nervous energy, it feels like being buried under a mountain. There are moments when everything becomes too much emotionally, mentally, and physically. This chapter is about those times. It's for when you feel overwhelmed, numb, hopeless, or scared and need a clear, gentle way forward.

Recognizing the Signs

Anxiety can build up slowly or hit like a wave. Either way, knowing the signs that you're reaching a breaking point is the first step to getting help.

Common warning signs:

- Feeling emotionally numb or hopeless

- Constant fatigue or trouble getting out of bed

- Loss of interest in things you used to enjoy

- Withdrawing from people, even those you love

- Intense irritability or crying spells

- Thoughts like "What's the point?" or "I can't do this anymore"

Key Insight:

Noticing these signs early gives you the chance to act before things get worse. You don't have to wait until you hit rock bottom.

When Anxiety Feels Like Too Much

Sometimes anxiety shows up as panic attacks, rapid heart rate, chest tightness, or racing thoughts. Other times it feels like you've shut down completely. Both responses are valid and both are signs that your nervous system is overwhelmed.

In these moments:

- Breathe slowly, even if it feels forced

- Name what's happening without judgment: "This is a panic attack," or "I feel frozen right now"

- Ground yourself with your five senses: what you can see, hear, touch, smell, and taste

Key Insight:

Your body and brain are trying to protect you, even if it doesn't feel that way.

Panic Attacks

Overthinking is one of the most common ways anxiety shows up, especially for teens. It's like your brain gets stuck on a loop, replaying the same scene over and over again, but instead of getting clearer, it just gets louder.

Maybe it's something you said in class, a message you sent to a friend, or a mistake you made on a quiz. You think about what happened, then about what could've happened, then about what might happen next. The worry spirals, and soon you're stuck in your head, feeling exhausted by thoughts that won't slow down.

This mental replaying often happens because your brain is trying to protect you. It wants to prepare for every possible outcome so you won't get caught off guard. But instead of helping, it ends up creating more stress. You might ask yourself "What if?" over and over *What if*

I fail? What if they don't like me? What if I mess up? These questions rarely lead to answers. Instead, they lead to more fear.

Overthinking doesn't just steal your focus, it drains your energy. It can make it hard to make decisions, because no choice feels safe. You might avoid speaking up in class or stop trying to fix a problem because your mind is too busy analyzing everything that could go wrong. Even simple tasks feel huge when your thoughts won't let you rest.

Sometimes, that overthinking builds up into something bigger: a panic attack. A panic attack can feel terrifying. Your heart might pound. Your chest might feel tight. You might get dizzy, shaky, or feel like you can't catch your breath. Some people feel like they're going to faint. Others feel like something terrible is about to happen, even if everything around them seems normal.

The important thing to know is panic attacks are not dangerous. They're uncomfortable, but they can't harm you. They're your body's way of responding to fear even if there's no clear reason why it's happening. In fact, panic attacks often come when there's been a lot of built-up anxiety that hasn't had a release. It's your nervous system hitting the emergency brakes because it thinks you're in danger, even if all you're doing is sitting in class or walking through the hallway.

One of the hardest parts of panic attacks is the fear of having another one. That fear can create more anxiety, leading to a cycle that's hard to break. But with the right tools like breathing techniques, grounding exercises, and calming self-talk, you can learn to manage them. You can train your body to recognize, *"This is a panic attack. It's not dangerous. It will pass."*

You are not your panic. You are not your thoughts. The storm may feel powerful in the moment, but you have more strength than you realize. Over time, with practice and support, you can quiet the noise and remind your mind and your body that you are safe.

Asking for Help (Even When It's Hard)

One of the bravest things you can do is say, "I'm not okay." Asking for help is not weakness it's strength.

People you can reach out to:

- A parent, guardian, or family member

- A school counselor, therapist, or coach

- A trusted teacher or mentor

- A close friend who listens without judgment

How to start the conversation:

- "I've been really struggling lately."

- "Can I talk to you about something personal?"

- "I think I need support, but I don't know where to start."

You don't need to explain everything just right. You just need to take the first step.

Key Insight:

You are not a burden. The people who care about you want to help even if they don't always know how right away.

Creating a Personal Crisis Plan

When you're in a high-stress or crisis moment, it can be hard to think clearly. Having a plan written out ahead of time can make all the difference.

What to include:

- Your signs that you're entering a crisis (e.g., thoughts, behaviors, physical symptoms)

- A list of safe people to call or text

- A list of grounding tools or coping strategies (breathing exercises, walking, journaling)

- Emergency contacts or hotlines (e.g., local crisis lines, 988 Suicide & Crisis Lifeline in the U.S.)

Write this plan down and keep it somewhere you can find easily: on your phone, in your journal, or taped to a mirror or notebook.

Staying Safe in the Moment

When anxiety becomes dangerous, for example if you're having thoughts of harming yourself, it's essential to prioritize safety.

Steps to take:

- Tell someone immediately even if it's just, "I'm scared."

- Remove or move away from anything that could be used to hurt yourself.

- Use grounding techniques, such as holding ice, feeling your feet on the floor, or   taking slow breaths.

- Reach out to crisis services or text a helpline if you can.

Key Insight:

There is always hope. Even when things feel impossible, support and safety are still possible.

Rebuilding After a Low Point

We all hit low points. Sometimes they come after a long buildup of stress and anxiety. Other times they show up unexpectedly, a panic attack out of nowhere, a failing grade we didn't see coming, a falling out with a close friend. Whatever the reason, these moments can leave us feeling defeated, hopeless, and unsure of what comes next. But here's the truth, low points are not the end of the story. They're the beginning of a new chapter one where you rebuild, grow, and rediscover your strength.

1. Accept Where You Are

The first step to rebuilding is acceptance. This doesn't mean giving up. It means acknowledging what you're feeling, without judgment. If you're overwhelmed, name it. If you're sad, tired, or scared, admit it to yourself. Avoiding or denying your emotions only gives them more power. Facing them head-on is how you begin to take it back.

Acceptance also means letting go of the pressure to bounce back quickly. Healing isn't linear. Some days will be better than others. Progress doesn't always look like constant improvement. It might look like getting out of bed when that feels hard. It might be texting a friend, finishing an assignment, or eating a meal. These are all real wins.

2. Get Grounded in the Present

After a low point, your mind might start to spiral rehashing mistakes, worrying about the future, or wondering what you should have done differently. But you can't heal in the past or the future. You can only heal in the present.

Start with grounding. Focus on your senses. What do you see around you? What sounds do you hear? Take slow breaths. Wiggle your fingers and toes. Name five things you can touch. These small acts bring you back to now and now is where you begin again.

Mindfulness tools like journaling, meditation, or simply sitting quietly with your thoughts gives you space to process what happened without being consumed by it. It helps you observe your emotions instead of being swept up in them.

3. Reconnect with Yourself

Low points can make you feel disconnected from who you are. You might question your identity or what matters to you. That's normal. Part of rebuilding is reconnecting with yourself beyond what went wrong.

Ask yourself:

What do I enjoy?

What brings me comfort?

Who helps me feel safe or seen?

Even small moments, such as watching a favorite show, a walk outside, or listening to music, that reclaim pieces of yourself. These aren't distractions. They're pieces of the puzzle that remind you who you are.

You can also use this time to explore new activities. Try experimenting with art, learning something new, drawing or writing. Each time you engage in something that feels good or meaningful, you lay another brick in your foundation.

4. Let Others In

One of the hardest things after a low point is feeling isolated. You might think no one will understand, or you might be afraid of being a burden. But connection is part of healing.

You don't have to share everything at once. Start with one persona trusted friend, a family member, a counselor. Say something simple: "I'm going through a tough time," or "I've been feeling really low lately." You might be surprised how many people are willing to support you.

Community, even in small doses, helps you feel less alone. Whether it's talking to someone face-to-face, joining an online group, or reading about others who've gone through similar things, connection reminds you that you're not the only one struggling and that support is real.

5. Focus on Small Steps

Rebuilding doesn't require a grand plan. You don't need to know exactly where you're going to start moving. Just pick one thing you can do today. Then another tomorrow.

Maybe it's making your bed. Drinking water. Showing up to class, even if you feel off. Each step proves to your brain that you're capable and still moving forward. Over time, small steps lead to big change.

You can even create a "recovery routine." This might include:

- A morning grounding activity (like deep breathing or stretching)

- One positive interaction (texting a friend, smiling at someone)

- One accomplishment (homework, cleaning, journaling)

- One moment of rest or enjoyment

It's not about perfection. It's about momentum.

6. Change the Story You Tell Yourself

Your inner narrative shapes how you see your life. After a low point, it's easy to slip into stories like "I'm a failure," or "Nothing will get better," but these stories aren't facts. They're interpretations and you have the power to shift them.

Try this:

- Identify the thought: "I messed everything up."

- Challenge it: Is that completely true? Did you *really* mess up everything?

- Reframe it: "I made a mistake, but I'm learning from it."

Over time, changing your self-talk helps you build resilience. You start to see yourself not as defeated, but as someone who's been through hard things and is still standing. That mindset is powerful.

7. Recognize Your Progress

Progress may feel slow, but it is there. Take time to reflect on what you've already survived. The low point didn't break you. You're still here, still trying, still growing. Celebrate that, keep a journal of small wins. Note the moments you spoke kindly to yourself, showed up when you didn't want to, or felt a little more like "you." Progress is not always a loud victory. Sometimes, it's a quiet return to yourself. You may not have chosen the low point, but you *do* get to choose how you rise from it. Rebuilding is possible. It starts with one breath, one step, one choice at a time. Keep going your future self is already proud of you. The path back from a dark place isn't always fast or straight but it is possible.

Tips for healing:

- Take one small step each day, such as showering, texting a friend or taking a walk

- Be gentle with your expectations

- Celebrate small victories, including, "I got through today"

- Reconnect with people or activities that bring light into your life

Reflection Questions:

1. What are your personal signs that things are becoming too heavy?

2. Who are 2–3 people you can reach out to in a crisis?

3. What does your calming or safety plan look like?

Action Step:

Create a written "When I'm Overwhelmed" plan. Include your signs, strategies, and support people. Review and update it regularly so you feel prepared when anxiety feels heavy.

CHAPTER 14

BUILDING A SUPPORT SYSTEM

One of the most powerful tools for managing stress, pressure, and anxiety is having a support system. Whether it's a trusted adult, a kind friend, or an online space that makes you feel seen, knowing you have backup can shift everything.

What Is a Support System?

A support system is more than just a group of people who are "there for you." It's a personal safety net, a team of trusted individuals who remind you that you don't have to face hard things by yourself. Whether you're dealing with stress, anxiety, disappointment, or even celebrating a win, your support system helps you process life in a healthier way. And the best part? You get to decide who's in it.

Think of your support system like different players on a team. Some might offer emotional support like a friend who listens without judgment. Others might help with practical things, like a teacher who gives you an extension on an assignment when you're overwhelmed. Some might be people you turn to just to laugh, vent, or take a break from your thoughts. No two support systems look the same, because your needs are unique.

A **strong support system** includes different kinds of connections:

- **Family members** who care about your well-being.

- **Friends** who accept you for who you are.

- **Mentors**, like teachers, coaches, or spiritual leaders, who encourage your growth.

- **Mental health professionals** who offer tools and guidance.

- **Online or peer support groups** where you feel seen and understood.

What makes someone part of a support system isn't how long you've known them, it's how safe they feel. A safe person listens when you need to talk, respects your boundaries, and doesn't make you feel ashamed of your emotions. They won't always have the answers, but they'll be present. Sometimes, just knowing someone cares can be enough to calm your nervous system.

Here's a secret: **even one supportive person can make a huge difference**.

Support systems aren't about being dependent they're about building healthy interdependence. Life is easier when you don't carry everything by yourself. It's also okay if your support system changes over time. Maybe you grow closer to one person and drift away from another. Maybe you're just now starting to build one. The important part is that you're open to connection, and you're learning to spot the people who make you feel heard, supported, and encouraged not drained or judged.

Creating a support system starts with small steps. You might begin by opening up to one person about how you're really feeling or by setting a boundary with someone who hasn't been supportive. You might even write a list of people who make you feel safe, and keep it somewhere you can see.

In a world where anxiety can make you feel isolated, a support system is your reminder that you're not alone. You don't have to figure everything out by yourself. You just need to know who to turn to and believe that you're worthy of support in the first place.

Opening Up the Conversation

One of the most powerful things you can do when you're struggling with anxiety is talk about it. Yet, for many teens, this is also one of the hardest steps to take. You might worry about being judged, misunderstood, or brushed off. You might feel like your struggles aren't "bad enough" to talk about or that no one will really understand what you're going through. But here's the truth, you are not the only one feeling like this.

When you keep everything inside, your thoughts can spiral, your emotions can build up, and it can start to feel like you're completely alone. But when you start to talk about what you're feeling, that silence breaks. The moment you speak up, even if it's just a few words, you create space for support, for understanding, and for healing.

Opening up doesn't mean announcing everything to the world. It starts small. It could be as simple as saying to a friend, "I've been really anxious lately." Or telling a parent, "I haven't been feeling like myself." It could even start with writing your thoughts in a journal, just to practice expressing what you're going through. The goal isn't to tell *everyone* just to let *someone* in.

Here's what often surprises people, when you open up, others often open up too. You may discover that your friend also struggles with anxiety, or that your teacher understands more than you thought. The more we normalize talking about mental health, the more it becomes okay to ask for help. Your voice might be the one that gives someone else the courage to speak up too.

Still, it's important to choose safe people to talk to. Not everyone will respond in the way you need. That doesn't mean you shouldn't talk, it just means you deserve someone who will listen without judgment.

A trusted adult, school counselor, therapist, coach, or even an online support group can be a great place to start. If talking feels too hard, you can write a note, send a message, or show someone this book and say, "This is how I've been feeling."

Opening up isn't about being dramatic or making a scene. It's about being real and giving yourself the support, you deserve. It's a brave move, and it often becomes the turning point in how you manage anxiety, and once the conversation starts, you may find that help, understanding, and relief were closer than you thought. Let that conversation be your first step toward feeling better for real.

When to Talk to Someone

Knowing *when* to talk to someone can be one of the hardest and most important parts of managing anxiety. There's often a voice in your head saying, *"It's not that bad,"* or *"Other people have it worse,"* or even *"I should be able to handle this on my own."* But the truth is, needing support is human. Talking to someone doesn't mean you're broken it means you're taking your mental health seriously.

So how do you know when it's time to reach out?

Start by tuning into how anxiety is showing up in your life. Is it keeping you from sleeping, eating, or concentrating? Are you skipping activities you normally enjoy? Do you feel like you're constantly on edge or exhausted from pretending everything is okay? These are signs that anxiety has moved from being a normal stress response into something that's impacting your daily functioning.

You don't have to wait until things are unbearable. In fact, talking to someone early before a full meltdown or shutdown can prevent things from getting worse. It's like going to the doctor when you first notice pain, instead of waiting until the injury becomes serious. Your emotional well-being works the same way. A good rule of thumb is this, if your anxiety is making life harder to manage, it's time to talk.

Here are a few signs it might be time to reach out:

- You feel stuck in a loop of worry that won't turn off.

- You're avoiding people, school, or responsibilities more often.

- You cry more easily or feel numb to everything.

- You're having trouble sleeping, eating, or taking care of yourself.

111

- You're having thoughts that scare you or feel out of control.

But it doesn't always have to be that intense. Maybe you just feel *off*. You're not sure what's wrong, but you know something doesn't feel right. That's reason enough. Who you talk to matters, too. Choose someone who listens without rushing to judge or fix.

You might worry about being a burden, but the people who care about you *want* to help. They can't support you if they don't know what you're going through. Opening up gives others the chance to show up for you in ways you didn't even know were possible.

And if the first person you talk to doesn't respond well? Try again. Their reaction is not a reflection of your worth it just means they weren't the right person for this moment.

Talking to someone doesn't solve everything overnight, but it starts the process. It builds a bridge between isolation and connection. And sometimes, that first conversation is the moment when things begin to shift. Not because you suddenly have all the answers but because you finally let someone walk beside you while you look for them.

Getting Comfortable Asking for Help

You don't need the perfect words. A simple "I don't feel okay" is enough to start the conversation. Courage doesn't always feel bold it often feels quiet and shaky. But it counts.

A support system is a network of people and resources you can turn to when you need help, encouragement, or just someone to listen. It's not about having dozens of friends or telling everyone everything it's about finding a few reliable, safe people you can lean on.

Qualities of a supportive person:

- Listens without judgment
- Respects your boundaries
- Encourages you to be yourself
- Doesn't try to "fix" you, but walks with you

Key Insight:

It's okay if your support system is small. Trust and safety matter more than the number of people.

Identifying the Safe People in Your Life

Start by taking inventory of who in your life feels safe to talk to. Ask yourself:

- Do they listen to me?

- Do I feel better, not worse, after talking to them?

- Have they respected my privacy in the past?

Your support people might include:

- Parents or guardians

- Teachers, counselors, or school staff

- Friends who show up consistently

- Mentors, coaches, or community leaders

Key Insight:

You don't need someone to understand everything you're going through. You need someone who's willing to try.

How to Strengthen Your Support System

Support systems are built, not born. Here's how to deepen trust and connection with the people in your life.

1. Start Small

- You don't have to pour out your whole story. Begin by opening up about something small and see how they respond.

2. Ask for What You Need

- "Can you just listen right now?"

- "I don't need advice, I just need support."

- "Would you be okay checking in with me sometimes?"

3. Show Up for Others, Too

- Support is a two-way street. Being a good listener helps strengthen bonds on both sides.

4. Check in Regularly

- Even a simple "Hey, thinking of you" text can keep your connections strong.

Online vs. In-Person Support

The internet can be a double-edged sword. Online spaces can connect you with people who understand but they can also increase anxiety, comparison, and misinformation.

When using online support:

- Stick to platforms that focus on mental health or positivity

- Avoid toxic comment sections or unmoderated forums

- Don't compare your healing journey to someone else's post

Offline connections offer eye contact, physical presence, and warmth. Try to balance both.

Key Insight:

Connection is a human need. Setting Healthy Boundaries Not everyone will be helpful, and that's okay. Part of building a strong support system is protecting your emotional energy.

You have the right to:

- Say no to people who make you feel worse

- Walk away from gossip or drama

- Choose what you share and with whom

Boundaries help you feel safer, not isolated.

Reflection Questions:

1. Who currently supports you, and how do they help?

2. Who might you like to build a stronger connection with?

3. What boundary do you need to set to feel safer in your relationships?

Action Step:

Make a support map. Write your name in the center of a page. Around it, add names of safe people and the kind of support they offer. Include digital spaces, mentors, and even pets or comfort items if they help you feel grounded. Let this visual remind you: You're not alone.

CHAPTER 15

SOCIAL MEDIA & SELF-IMAGE

Social media is a major part of most teens' lives. It's where you connect, express yourself, and stay in the loop. But it can also be a major trigger for anxiety, especially when it comes to self-image and feeling like you don't measure up. In this chapter, we'll explore the connection between digital life and mental health and how to protect your peace while staying connected.

Comparison Culture

It's natural to look around and compare yourself to others. It's part of how humans learn, we observe, notice differences, and try to make sense of where we stand. But in today's world, comparison isn't just a once-in-a-while thing. It's constant. It's passive. And thanks to social media, it happens all day long.

Over time, this kind of daily comparison starts to chip away at your self-worth. You begin to question whether you're doing enough, achieving enough, or even *being* enough. It becomes easy to feel like everyone else is happier, prettier, more popular, or more successful. The result? You feel like you're falling behind in a race you didn't even choose to run.

Comparison culture can create anxiety in ways that are subtle but powerful. You might start obsessing over your looks, questioning your friendships, or pushing yourself to succeed in ways that don't even feel right for you. Instead of tuning in to what *you* value, you start chasing what looks impressive online. That disconnect between who you really are and who you think you should be? That's where anxiety festers.

To break free from comparison, you first have to *notice* when it's happening. Become aware of the thoughts that pop up when you scroll, "I wish I looked like that," "Why don't I have a relationship like theirs?" or "I'll never be as good as them." These aren't facts, they're judgments rooted in someone else's story, not your own.

Remember comparison steals joy. It shifts your focus from progress to perfection, from growth to guilt. But when you center your life around your own values, goals, and pace, you begin to build confidence that isn't based on how you stack up, but on who you truly are. Your journey doesn't need to look like anyone else's to be meaningful. Keep your eyes on your own path and you'll go much further.

How comparison hurts:

- You start believing your life isn't enough

- You feel pressure to look or act a certain way

- You lose touch with what really matters to you

Signs it's time for a break:

- You feel worse after being online

- You constantly check your likes or followers

- You're more focused on your image than your real life

Reclaiming Your Feed

Steps to take:

- Unfollow or mute accounts that trigger insecurity

- Set screen time limits or app timers

- Ask yourself: "Do I feel better or worse after using this app?"

Building Real Confidence Offline

Likes are not love. Follows are not friendship. True self-image is built off-screen.

How to build self-worth IRL:

- Keep promises to yourself

- Pursue hobbies that make you feel proud

- Surround yourself with people who see your worth beyond your appearance

- Journal about your wins and what makes you, you

Key Insight:

Your value isn't something others decide it's something you build and protect.

Reflection Questions:

1. What emotions do you usually feel after being on social media?

2. Who or what on your feed supports your mental health?

3. What would you like to see more or less of in your digital life?

Action Step:

Audit your social media feed. Go through your accounts and ask, "Does this make me feel good about myself?" Curate your space to match your values, goals, and wellbeing not anyone else's highlight reel.

CHAPTER 16

YOUR PERSONALIZED ANXIETY TOOLKIT

Managing anxiety isn't about finding one perfect strategy it's about building a set of tools that work for you. Just like every person is unique, your anxiety management plan should reflect your preferences, lifestyle, and needs. This chapter guides you through assembling a go-to toolkit you can rely on during anxious moments and everyday stress.

What Is an Anxiety Toolkit?

An anxiety toolkit is a collection of coping skills, habits, reminders, and resources that help ground you when anxiety shows up. Think of it like a mental health first-aid kit ready to use when you need it.

What it might include:

- Breathing exercises or grounding techniques

- Journal prompts or affirmation cards

- Safe people to contact

- A comfort object or fidget tool

- Your favorite calming playlist

Key Insight:

Your toolkit doesn't have to be fancy it just has to work for you.

Daily Anxiety Management Tools

The more consistently you use your toolkit, the stronger your coping muscle becomes.

1. Morning Grounding Routine

- Start the day with intention
- Use a 5-minute breathing or stretching session
- Set a positive focus or affirmation for the day

2. Midday Check-In

- Pause and ask, "What do I need right now?"
- Use a grounding technique such as 5-4-3-2-1 or body scan
- Take a movement break or hydration break

3. Evening Wind-Down

- Write in a journal or reflect on one win from your day
- Unplug from screens at least 30 minutes before bed
- Use a calming practice like deep breathing or quiet reading

Tools for High-Stress Moments

Anxiety doesn't wait for a convenient time. That's why having "in-the-moment" tools ready is essential.

- Coping Cards: Write down 3 things that calm you, 3 truths to remember, and 3 people you can contact.

- Anxiety Box: A small box with sensory items like soft fabric, essential oils, a calming quote, or stress toys.

- Safe Spaces List: Know where you can go to regroup, library, quiet hallway, counselor's office, or a nature spot.

Key Insight:

Having a plan ahead of time helps you feel more in control during stressful moments.

Personalizing Your Plan

To make your toolkit truly helpful, it must reflect your preferences, not someone else's suggestions.

1. Know What Works

- Look back at previous chapters. Which techniques helped?

- Highlight or bookmark strategies you want to try again.

2. Adjust as You Grow

- Your needs change. So, should your toolkit.

- Swap tools in and out depending on your season or setting.

3. Keep It Accessible

- Create a note on your phone titled "My Toolkit"

- Use a pouch or box for physical tools in your backpack

- Make a visual version on a journal page or whiteboard

Celebrating Progress

Don't wait for perfection to celebrate your growth. Every time you use your toolkit even if it doesn't fix everything is a win.

Ways to track progress:

- Keep a "Bravery Log" of moments you faced anxiety head-on

- Reflect weekly on what worked and what you want to try differently

- Reward yourself for showing up for yourself consistently

Key Insight

You don't need to be anxiety-free to feel proud. Managing it is the win.

Reflection Questions:

1. What tools have helped you the most when feeling anxious?

2. What are three small things you can add to your daily routine to feel more grounded?

3. Where can you keep your toolkit so it's always within reach?

Action Step:

Create your personalized anxiety toolkit. Write down or gather:

- 3 calming strategies you've learned in this book

- 3 supportive people you can reach out to

- 3 reminders that make you feel strong

Use your toolkit as often as needed. The more you reach for it, the more it becomes second nature. You've built something powerful now trust yourself to use it.

CONCLUSION + RESOURCES

If you've made it to the end of this book pause and acknowledge that. You've just taken a meaningful step toward understanding your anxiety and building the tools to navigate it. That's not a small thing. That's the kind of work that shapes a stronger, wiser, and more grounded version of you.

You're Not Alone

Anxiety might try to convince you that you're isolated or different, but millions of teens are walking a similar path. The more we speak openly about mental health, the more we normalize getting help, setting boundaries, and choosing healing.

Whether your anxiety is mild or intense, occasional or persistent, the key is not to go it alone. You now have tools, awareness, and options. Most importantly, you have a future that's worth caring for.

Use the Tools Don't Just Read Them

Come back to the chapters that helped you. Reread a technique before a big exam, a social situation, or a stressful week. Use the reflection questions in your journal. Carry your toolkit with you mentally or physically.

Key Insight:

Healing isn't about avoiding anxiety, it's about learning how to live well alongside it.

Helpful Resources

Whether you're ready to go deeper or just want to know where to turn next, here are some resources for teens experiencing anxiety:

Emergency Support

- National Suicide & Crisis Lifeline (U.S.): Dial or text 988

- Crisis Text Line: Text HOME to 741741

- Emergency Services: 911 if you or someone is in immediate danger

Online Support & Education

- Teen Mental Health: teenmentalhealth.org

- Youth Anxiety Resources: jack.org

- Anxiety and Depression Association of America (ADAA): adaa.org

Apps That Support Mental Health

- Calm (mindfulness & meditation)

- Headspace (stress & sleep support)

- Moodpath or Sanvello (mood tracking and CBT tools)

Final Words

This book isn't meant to be a one-time read, it's a toolkit. Reuse it. Revisit it. Rewrite parts of it in your own words. Most importantly, believe in your ability to handle life, one small moment at a time. You're already doing the work.

That matters more than you know.

Aisha Broadwater, PhD